See the **WIDER** picture

Sky lanterns at Yee Peng Festival, Chiangmai, Thailand

The people of Chiang Mai celebrate the Yee Peng Festival every year. The festival usually happens in November when there is a full moon. The local people believe this is the perfect time to wish for good luck. They make a wish and launch a "Khom Loi" lantern into the sky. Thousands of lanterns across the night sky is a very beautiful sight.

What would you wish for?

Course Map

Your Student's Book comes with access to:

▶ The Student's eBook

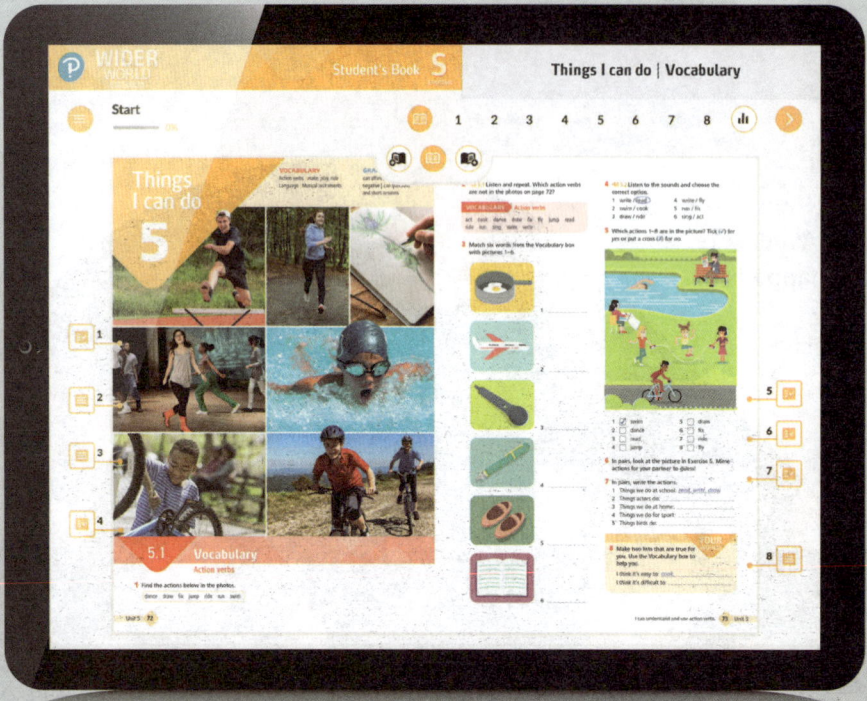
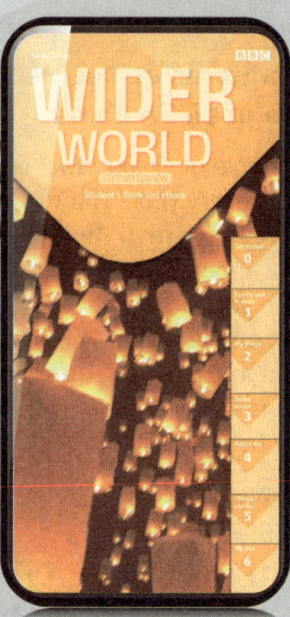

Audio, video and interactive activities with instant marking bring the content of the Student's Book to life in the eBook. It includes everything you need to participate in online lessons.

Wider World Second Edition is fully accessible on your computer, tablet and mobile phone. You can enjoy the full functionality of your course wherever you are.

You can access your digital components through the Pearson English Portal. See the inside front cover for access details.

Classroom Lessons

Student's Book

Workbook

Online Lessons

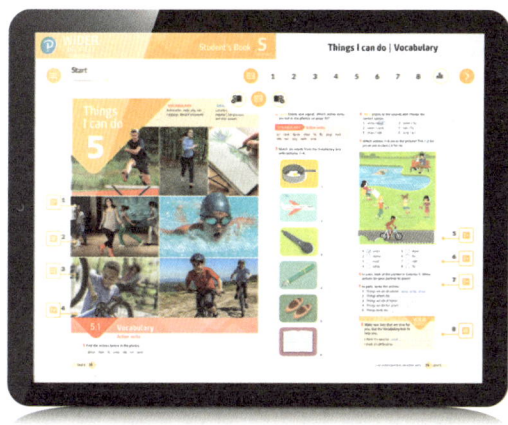
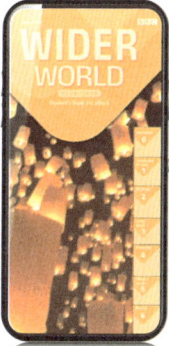

eBook

Homework

Workbook

Contents

		Vocabulary	Grammar	Grammar	Speaking
Get started! 0		**0.1 How do you spell that?** The alphabet | Spelling words/names | I'm … | I like | He/She likes … | This is … pp. 6–7		**0.2 Numbers and colours** Numbers | Colours pp. 8–9	
Family and friends 1		• Family • Possessive 's pp. 12–13	VIDEO ▶ *It's Granny's birthday!* • to be affirmative • my, your pp. 14–15	The Terrific Two – Dug's family album • to be negative • Countries and nationalities pp. 16–17	VIDEO ▶ *Nice to meet you!* Introductions p. 18
		BBC CULTURE English around the world	VIDEO ▶ This is the UK		
My things 2		• Clothes pp. 26–27	VIDEO ▶ *That's my T-shirt!* • this, that, these, those • Adjectives p. 28–29	The Terrific Two – Dug's new suit • to be questions and short answers pp. 30–31	VIDEO ▶ *What's your name?* Asking for personal information p. 32
		SET FOR LIFE Collaboration Make decisions as a group Great idea! pp. 38–39			
In the house 3		• In the house pp. 42–43	VIDEO ▶ *There's a phone on the sofa!* • there is/there are affirmative • Prepositions of place pp. 44–45	The Terrific Two – Dug and Coco • there is/there are negative and questions pp. 46–47	VIDEO ▶ *Where's the bathroom?* Having a guest p. 48
		BBC CULTURE What do houses look like in the UK?	VIDEO ▶ Hampton Court Palace		
About me 4		• Face, eyes, hair pp. 56–57	VIDEO ▶ *I haven't got big feet!* • have got affirmative and negative • Parts of the body pp. 58–59	The Terrific Two – My favourite superhero! • have got questions and short answers pp. 60–61	VIDEO ▶ *Sorry about that!* Apologising p. 62
		SET FOR LIFE Self-management Being organised Keeping things tidy pp. 68–69			
Things I can do 5		• Action verbs pp. 72–73	VIDEO ▶ *I can fix it!* • can affirmative and negative • make, play, ride pp. 74–75	The Terrific Two – Thank you, Superdug! • can questions and short answers pp. 76–77	VIDEO ▶ *Let's do something fun!* Suggestions p. 78
		BBC CULTURE Young London	VIDEO ▶ Free-time activities		
My day 6		• Daily activities pp. 86–87	VIDEO ▶ *I listen to classical music.* • Present Simple affirmative pp. 88–89	The Terrific Two – Dug's busy week • Adverbs of frequency • Days of the week pp. 90–91	VIDEO ▶ *The film starts at four o'clock.* Telling the time p. 92
		SET FOR LIFE Environmental responsibility Repairing things or recycling them Give things a new life! pp. 98–99			
Animals 7		• Wild animals pp. 102–103	VIDEO ▶ *I don't like cats!* • Present Simple negative • Pets pp. 104–105	The Terrific Two – Superdug's interview • Present Simple questions and short answers pp. 106–107	VIDEO ▶ *One ticket, please.* Buying a ticket p. 108
		BBC CULTURE Pets in the UK	VIDEO ▶ London Zoo		
I like that! 8		• Sports pp. 116–117	VIDEO ▶ *Let's go to summer camp!* • love / like / don't like / hate + -ing • Object pronouns pp. 118–119	The Terrific Two – Dug's sports hero • Question words pp. 120–121	VIDEO ▶ *What's the weather like?* Talking about the weather p. 122
		SET FOR LIFE Leadership Reacting to mistakes I'm sorry, it's my fault! pp. 128–129			

GRAMMAR TIME pp. 132–139   STUDENT ACTIVITIES pp. 140–142

0.3 In the classroom
Classroom objects | Classroom language
pp. 10–11

Reading and Vocabulary	Listening and Writing	CLIL	Revision	Progress Check
Family photo album A blog post about a family • Places p. 19	*Best friends* Listening: A podcast about best friends Writing: A blog post about your best friend • Capital letters p. 20	Art: *Families in Art.* • Art p. 21	Vocabulary Activator p. 22 Revision p. 23	**1–2** pp. 40–41 • Vocabulary and Grammar: open cloze • Speaking: answering questions • Listening: answering questions • Reading: answering questions • Writing: a short text about you and your family
Project: A digital presentation of a country pp. 24–25				
My things An article about a gadget • My things p. 33	*My favourite things* Listening: A dialogue about people and their things Writing: A blog post about your favourite things • Punctuation p. 34	Geometry: *Shapes* • Shapes p. 35	Vocabulary Activator p. 36 Revision p. 37	
A dream house A text about a skateboarder's dream house • Household objects p. 49	*My bedroom* Listening: Descriptions of bedrooms Writing: A blog post about your bedroom • Apostrophes p. 50	Science: *Materials* • Materials p. 51	Vocabulary Activator p. 52 Revision p. 53	**1–4** pp. 70–71 • Vocabulary and Grammar: multiple choice, open cloze • Speaking: multiple choice, describing your favourite room in your house and your favourite person in your family • Listening: matching • Reading: multiple matching, True/False • Writing: a description of your favourite place
Project: A digital presentation of interesting or unusual houses all over the world pp. 54–55				
Personality quiz A quiz about personalities • Personality adjectives p. 63	*Your favourite cartoon character* Listening: A description of favourite cartoon characters Writing: A description of your favourite cartoon character • Paragraphs p. 64	Science: *Genes* • Adjectives p. 65	Vocabulary Activator p. 66 Revision p. 67	
Sign language A text about sign language • Language p. 79	*After-school clubs* Listening: People talking about after-school clubs Writing: An ad for an after-school club • Linkers: *and, but* p. 80	Music: *Musical instruments* • Musical instruments p. 81	Vocabulary Activator p. 82 Revision p. 83	**1–6** pp. 100–101 • Vocabulary and Grammar: multiple choice, open cloze • Speaking: multiple matching, answering questions • Reading: multiple choice, answering questions • Listening: multiple choice • Writing: a text about what you do on holiday
Project: A promotional email about the fun things visitors can do in your area pp. 84–85				
Interview with a traveller A text about a teenager's unusual life • Months p. 93	*A typical weekend* Listening: A dialogue about friends and what they are doing Writing: A blog post about your typical weekend • *before, after* p. 94	Technology: *The internet* • On the internet p. 95	Vocabulary Activator p. 96 Revision p. 97	
Amazing animals A text about three animals • Adjectives p. 109	*Looking after a pet* Listening: A radio interview with a pet expert Writing: An email asking someone to look after your pet • Starting and ending an email p. 110	Science: *The environment* • Where animal live p. 111	Vocabulary Activator p. 112 Revision p. 113	**1–8** pp. 130–131 • Vocabulary and Grammar: matching, open cloze • Listening: matching • Speaking: mini dialogues • Reading and Writing: matching texts with photos, completing a table, cloze • Writing: a text about your favourite sport
Project: A digital presentation with photos and information about your ideal pets pp. 114–115				
Healthy lifestyle Top tips for a healthy lifestyle • Healthy lifestyle p. 123	*Your lifestyle* Listening: Two interviews with young athletes Writing: A blog post about your lifestyle • Checking grammar p. 124	Sports: *Sports equipment* • Sports equipment p. 125	Vocabulary Activator p. 126 Revision p. 127	

Get started!

0

VOCABULARY
The alphabet | Spelling words/names | Numbers | Colours | Classroom objects | Classroom language

GRAMMAR
I'm … |
I like / He/She likes … |
This is …

Hi, I'm Jen Newman. I'm ten years old. I like cupcakes!

Hi, I'm Alex. I'm twelve. I like computers and computer games.

I'm Lian and I'm twelve. I like skateboarding. I like all sports.

Hello. I'm Lucas. I'm from Spain. I like music and Maths.

I'm Miranda Newman.

And I'm Larry Newman. We're Jen and Alex's mum and dad!

0.1 How do you spell that?

1. ▶ 1 🔊 0.2 Watch the video. Then listen and read. Who is twelve?

2. Look at the photos and read. Complete the sentences.
   1. Jen likes *cupcakes*.
   2. Alex likes computers and _____.
   3. Lian likes all _____.
   4. Lucas likes _____ and Maths.

Unit 0 6

3 Play a game! Stand in a line. Ask and answer.
A: I'm Mario. What's your name?
B: I'm Ella. What's your name?
C: My name's David. …

4 🔊 0.3 🔊 0.4 **Listen and do the Alphabet Rap.**

, , , D,
E, F, G,

Say the alphabet, say it with me!

H, I, J, K, L, M, N, O, P,

 is funny, as you can see.

R, S, T, U and V,

Four more letters and we're free.

W, X, Y and – shh …

 is sleepy, so are we!

5 Complete the words with the letters below. Say the letters.

t f g x l s

1 irl

2 bo __

3 __ andwich

4 __ able

5 __ ion

6 __ ish

6 🔊 0.5 **Listen and tick (✓) the letters you hear.**

1	A ✓	E ✓	I ☐
2	G ☐	J ☐	C ☐
3	W ☐	U ☐	Y ☐
4	B ☐	D ☐	P ☐
5	M ☐	N ☐	F ☐
6	I ☐	J ☐	Y ☐

7 Work in pairs. Say the alphabet. Stop when the teacher tells you. Your partner says what comes next.

A, B, C, D, …   Stop!   E!

WATCH OUT!
LL = double L

8 🔊 0.6 Listen and complete the names. In pairs, compare your answers.
1 H A I L E Y
2 B __ T __ Y
3 __ E __ __ A L
4 __ I __ L __ A __

9 Work in pairs. Ask for your partner's name. Write it down.
A: What's your name?
B: Vicky.
A: How do you spell that?
B: V-I-C-K-Y. Vicky.

YOUR WORLD

10 Have a class spelling competition.

Music. M-U-S-I-C. Music.

I can say and spell my name.

0.2 Numbers and colours

The Terrific Two – Meet Dug and Kit

This is Dug. Dug is also Superdug. Superdug is a superhero.

This is Kit. Kit is very clever. She is Dug's best friend.

1 🔊 0.7 Listen and read. Look at the picture. Choose the correct option.

Dug / Kit is a superhero.

2 🔊 0.8 In pairs, listen and point. Say who they are.

Coco   Granny   Kit   Roberto   Superdug   Wonder Will

This is Superdug.

3 🔊 0.9 Listen and repeat.

VOCABULARY	Numbers 1–12	
1 one	5 five	9 nine
2 two	6 six	10 ten
3 three	7 seven	11 eleven
4 four	8 eight	12 twelve

4 Complete the numbers.

1 o _n_ e
2 __ w __
3 t _ r __ __
4 __ o __ r
5 f __ __ e
6 __ i __
7 __ e __ e __
8 e i __ __ t
9 __ i n __
10 t __ __

5 Write the answer in words.

1 six + six = _twelve_
2 ten − one = _____
3 two + three = _____
4 twelve − nine = _____
5 two − one = _____
6 two + six = _____
7 five + two = _____
8 twelve − one = _____

6 🔊 0.10 Listen and repeat.

VOCABULARY	Numbers 13–20
13 thirteen	17 seventeen
14 fourteen	18 eighteen
15 fifteen	19 nineteen
16 sixteen	20 twenty

7 Choose the correct number.
1 four — ④ / 14
2 fifteen — 5 / 15
3 thirteen — 3 / 13
4 eight — 8 / 18
5 twenty — 2 / 20
6 seven — 7 / 17

8 🔊 0.11 Listen and write the number.
a _20_   e _____
b _____   f _____
c _____   g _____
d _____   h _____

9 🔊 0.12 Listen and repeat.

VOCABULARY Colours

black   blue   green   red   white   yellow

10 Look at Exercise 4. Write the numbers which are this colour.
red _1, 8_   yellow _____
blue _____   black _____
green _____

11 Play a game! Student A, listen to Student B and guess. Then change roles.
A: What's your favourite colour?
B: Not white, not yellow, not green, not blue, not black.
A: It's red!

12 Look at the picture below. Match 1–5 with a–e.
1 The flowers are   a blue.
2 The zebras are   b yellow.
3 The sky is   c red.
4 The lemons are   d green.
5 The trees are   e black and white.

13 Play a game! Finish the sentences.
A: The trees are …
B: … red.
C: No! They're green. The pond is …
D: … blue!
E: Yes! The zebras are …

I can say numbers 1–20 and name basic colours.

0.3 In the classroom

1 🔊 0.13 Listen and repeat. Match the words in the Vocabulary box with objects A–F in Alex's bag.

VOCABULARY In my bag

book   notebook   pen   pencil   ruler   sandwich

WATCH OUT!
a pencil   six pencils
a sandwich   two sandwiches

2 Look at the pictures. How many things can you see?

1 *six notebooks*

2 _____

3 _____   4 _____

5 _____

3 🔊 0.14 Listen and repeat. Match the words in the Vocabulary box with objects A–E in the picture.

VOCABULARY Classroom objects

bin   board   chair   clock   desk

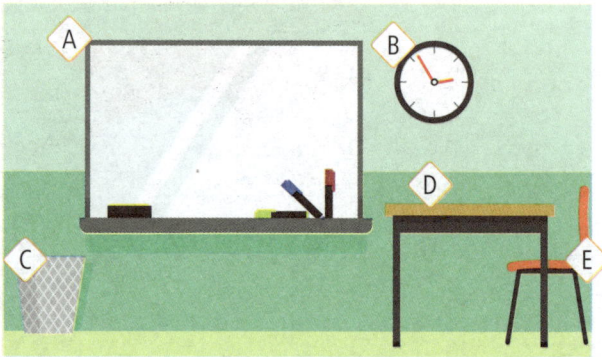

A _____   D _____
B _____   E _____
C _____

4 Find objects from the Vocabulary box in Exercise 3 in your classroom and point at them.

WATCH OUT!
It's a board.
They're desks.

5 In pairs, guess what these objects are. Then go to page 140 and check.

 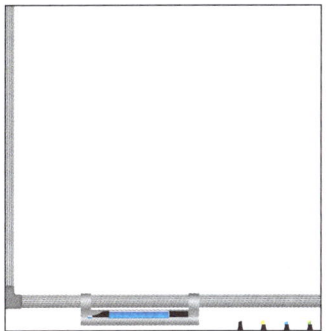

1 It's a _____ .   2 _____

3 _____   4 _____

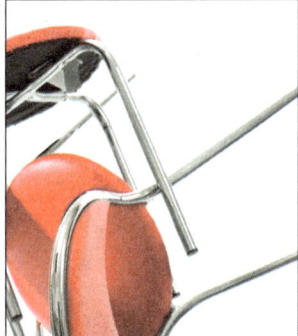 

5 _____   6 _____

6 🔊 0.15 Listen and repeat.

> **SPEAKING** Classroom language
>
> Open your books.
> Close your books.
> Listen (to the story).
> Look (at the photo).
> Read (the text).
> Write (your name).
> Sit down.
> Stand up.
> Work in pairs.
> Can you help me, please?
> Can you repeat that, please?
> What's … in English?

7 Read the expressions in the Speaking box again. Who usually says them: a teacher or a student?

> **WATCH OUT!**
> Can you help me, **please**?
> Stand up, **please**!

8 🔊 0.16 Match 1–4 with a–d. Listen and check. In pairs, act out the dialogues.

1 ☐ Can you repeat that, please?
2 ☐ Can you help me, Miss?
3 ☐ How do we say this word in English?
4 ☐ What does 'amazing' mean?

a We say 'elephant'.
b It means 'really good'.
c Yes, Maria. How can I help you?
d Yes, Thomas. Giraffe. Giraffe. OK?

YOUR WORLD

9 Play a game! Be a teacher. Tell other students what to do. Use the expressions in the Speaking box.

I can talk about classroom objects and understand classroom instructions.   **11** Unit 0

Family and friends

1

VOCABULARY
Family | Countries and nationalities | Places | Art

GRAMMAR
to be affirmative | *to be* negative | *my*, *your* | possessive *'s*

Vittorio

Agatha

Colin

Julia

Paul

Rosa

Tom

Anna

Mark

David

Evita

1.1 Vocabulary

Family

1 Read the words below. What do they mean?

brother dad daughter grandad granny mum sister son

Unit 1 12

2 🔊 **1.1 Listen and repeat.**

> **VOCABULARY** Family
>
> mother   mum   father   dad   parents
> grandfather   grandad   grandmother
> granny   son   daughter   brother   sister
> aunt   uncle   cousin

3 Complete the table with family words from the Vocabulary box.

He	She
father	*mother*
_____	grandmother
son	_____
_____	sister
uncle	_____
_____	cousin

4 Match 1–4 with a–d.
1 father   a grandad
2 grandmother   b dad
3 mother   c granny
4 grandfather   d mum

> ⚠️ **WATCH OUT!**
> Paul = Mark's father
> Evita = Rosa's daughter

5 Look at the family tree on page 12 and write the names.
1 Mark's grandfather   *Vittorio*
2 Mark's sister   _____
3 Mark's aunt   _____
4 Mark's cousins   _____
5 Mark's grandmother   _____

6 Look at the family tree on page 12 again. Complete each sentence with one of the names below.

> Colin's   Julia's   ~~Mark's~~
> Paul's   Rosa's   Tom's

1 Colin is *Mark's* uncle.
2 Julia is _____ sister.
3 David is _____ son.
4 Anna is _____ daughter.
5 Vittorio and Agatha are _____ parents.
6 Evita is _____ cousin.

7 🔊 **1.2 Listen and choose T (true) or F (false). Then listen again and check your answers.**

Vittorio   Anna
1 T / F   2 T / F

Julia   Agatha
3 T / F   4 T / F

Paul   Mark
5 T / F   6 T / F

> **YOUR WORLD**
>
> **8** Draw your family tree. Write the names of the people in your family.

I can talk about the people in a family.   **13**   Unit 1

1.2 Grammar
to be affirmative

VIDEO **IT'S GRANNY'S BIRTHDAY!**

Sophie is Jen and Alex's grandmother. Today is Sophie's birthday. She is seventy years old.

Sophie: I'm so happy you're here.

Alex: It's Aunt Megan!
Megan: Hello, Alex! Hold this, please. Be careful! It's Granny's birthday cake.
Alex: It's OK. I've got it!

Megan: Happy birthday, Mum! Here's your present.
Sophie: Thank you, my darling.
Dad: Hello, sister!

Dad: We're ready for the cake!
Mum: Oh, no!

1 ▶ 2 🔊 1.3 Watch the video. Then listen and read. Answer the question.

How old is Jen and Alex's granny today?

2 Read the sentences. Mark them T (true) or F (false). Correct the false sentences.
1 Granny isn't very happy. T / F
2 Granny's name is Sophie. T / F
3 There's a present for Alex in the box. T / F
4 Dad is Megan's brother. T / F

3 🔊 1.4 Listen and repeat. Find these expressions in the story.

SOUNDS GOOD! Hold this, please. • Be careful! • I've got it!

4 Jen and Alex's mum says 'Oh, no!' Why? Have a class vote. Choose the correct answer.
a The cake is a mess.
b It isn't Granny's cake.
c A mouse is in the box.

5 ▶ 3 🔊 1.5 Now watch or listen and check.

6 Study the Grammar box. Then watch.

GRAMMAR — *to be* affirmative

Long form	Short form
I am eleven.	I'm eleven.
You are eleven.	You're eleven.
He/She/It is eleven.	He/She/It's eleven.
We are eleven.	We're eleven.
You are eleven.	You're eleven.
They are eleven.	They're eleven.

VIDEO ▶ 4 GET GRAMMAR!

We're friends!

Hammy is my pet hamster.

7 Find the sentences in the story on page 14. Complete the sentences with the missing word.
1 She *is* seventy years old.
2 'I _____ so happy!'
3 'You _____ here!'
4 'It _____ Granny's birthday cake.'
5 'We _____ ready for the cake!'

8 Choose the correct option.
1 You *are* / *is* ready.
2 I *is* / *am* here.
3 We *am* / *are* happy!
4 It *are* / *is* a present for you.
5 They *is* / *are* at Granny's house.

9 Rewrite the sentences in Exercise 8 in your notebook, using the short form of the verb *to be*.
1 *You're ready.*

WATCH OUT!
I → my   It's **my** birthday. I'm ten!
you → your   It's **your** birthday. You're eleven!

10 Complete the sentences with *my* or *your*.
1 Alex: Granny, here's *your* birthday card!
2 Sophie: I'm very happy! _____ family is here!
3 Alex: _____ birthday cake is in this box, Granny.
4 Jen: Sophie is _____ granny too!

11 🔊 1.6 How old are they? Complete the sentences. Then listen and check.
1 Lucas: I'*m eleven*. — 10
2 Lian: Alex and I _____ . 16
3 Lucas: My brother _____ . 11
4 Lian to Jen: You _____ , right? 12

12 Complete the text with *am*, *are* or *is*.

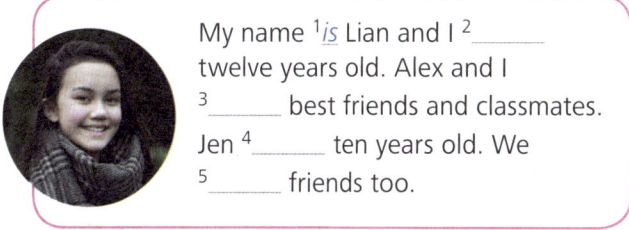

My name ¹*is* Lian and I ² _____ twelve years old. Alex and I ³ _____ best friends and classmates. Jen ⁴ _____ ten years old. We ⁵ _____ friends too.

13 Read the text in Exercise 12 again. Then write about you and your friends.
My name _____ and I _____ .

YOUR WORLD

14 Read the poem. Make changes to talk about a friend or classmate.

I'm **twelve** today,
Hip, hip, hooray!
Let's have a break
And eat some cake!

Kelly's thirteen today …

I can use the affirmative form of the verb *to be* and *my*, *your*.

1.3 Grammar
to be negative

The Terrific Two – Dug's family album

1 Look at the cartoon. How many types of dogs can you see?

2 🔊 **1.7** Listen and read. What nationality is Uncle Roberto?

3 Read the sentences. Mark them T (true) or F (false).
1. Uncle Roberto is a superhero. T / F
2. Aunt Gigi is French. T / F
3. Dug's parents are superheroes. T / F
4. Dug is happy in the photo. T / F
5. Dug's mum is British. T / F

4 Study the Grammar box. Then watch.

GRAMMAR — to be negative

Long form	Short form
I am not British.	I'm not British.
You are not British.	You aren't British.
He/She/It is not British.	He/She/It isn't British.
We are not British.	We aren't British.
You are not British.	You aren't British.
They are not British.	They aren't British.

VIDEO 5 GET GRAMMAR!

Hammy isn't orange.

No, I'm not orange and I'm not fat.

5 In your notebook, write negative sentences. Use the long form of the verb *to be*.
1 Dug is French.
   Dug is not French.
2 Kit is a dog.
3 Dug's parents are superheroes.
4 Dug: 'I am happy.'
5 Kit: 'You are in the photo, Dug.'
6 Dug is orange.

6 Rewrite the sentences in Exercise 5 in your notebook. Use the short form of the verb *to be*.
1 *Dug isn't French.*

7 🔊 1.8 Look, listen and repeat.

VOCABULARY — Countries and nationalities

- the UK / British
- Turkey / Turkish
- Spain / Spanish
- France / French
- Poland / Polish
- China / Chinese
- the USA / American

8 Look at the flags. Complete the sentences about Dug's family with *is* or *isn't*.
1 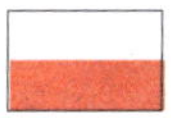 Aunt Teresa *isn't* Spanish. She *is Polish.*
2  Grandad Mateo _____ Chinese. He _____ .
3  Cousin Lulu _____ French.
4  Cousin Chen _____ British. He _____ .
5  Granny Flossie _____ American.

9 In your notebook, write sentences about Kit's friends and family.

I'm not from Turkey. I'm from the UK.

1 Turkey ✗ the UK ✓
We …

2 Spain ✗ the UK ✓
Granny Ola …

3 France ✗ Poland ✓
My cousins …

4 the USA ✗ China ✓

YOUR WORLD

10 Choose your nationality and play *Three Guesses*.
A: You're Spanish!
B: No, I'm not Spanish.
A: You're British!
B: No, I'm not British.
A: You're Turkish!
B: Yes, I'm Turkish.

1.4 Speaking
Introductions

VIDEO ▶ NICE TO MEET YOU!

Jen: Hi, Mum!
Mum: Hi, kids!
Jen: Mum, this is Lucas.
He's our new neighbour.
Lucas, this is my mum.
Mum: Hello, Lucas. Nice to meet you.
Lucas: Nice to meet you too, Mrs Newman.
Mum: Jen, your bag!
Jen: Sorry, Mum. Let's go, Lucas.

1 ▶ 6 🔊 1.9 Watch the video. Then listen and read. What is Jen's family name?

2 🔊 1.10 Listen and repeat.

> **SPEAKING Introductions**
>
> A: *Mum*, this is *Lucas*.
> *He* is my *friend/classmate*
> *Lucas*, this is *my mum*.
> B: Hello, *Lucas*. Nice to meet you.
> C: Nice to meet you too.

3 🔊 1.11 Put the dialogue in the correct order. Then listen and check.
1 *b*   2 ___   3 ___   4 ___

a Desi: Nice to meet you too, Lisa.
b Adam: Lisa, this is Desi. He's my best friend.
c Lisa: Hello, Desi. Nice to meet you.
d Adam: Desi, this is my cousin, Lisa.

4 In groups of three, act out the dialogue in Exercise 3.

5 Choose the best answer.
1 A: Hello, I'm George.
　B: a Very well, thanks.
　　　b I've got it!
　　　c Nice to meet you, George.
2 A: Mum, this is Sam.
　B: a He's my classmate.
　　　b Hello, Sam.
　　　c Hold this, please.
3 A: Kate, this is my sister, Lisa.
　B: a Be careful!
　　　b Hi, Lisa. Nice to meet you.
　　　c She's my friend.

YOUR WORLD

6 Write the names of three famous people. Then introduce them to your friends!

Talia, this is my friend, Emma Stone. She's a film star!

pop star _____
film star _____
sports star _____

Unit 1 18 I can make introductions.

1.5 Reading and Vocabulary
Family photo album

My family album
I'm Alice! I'm thirteen. I'm from London in the UK. This is my family album.

This is my favourite photo. I'm four and my sister Isabel is six. In this photo we are at my granny's house in London. Granny is Dad's mum. She's fun!

My cousin Tommy, Isabel and I are in this photo. I'm nine, Tommy's ten and Isabel's eleven.

And this is my family: Mum, Dad, Isabel and me. I'm eleven and Isabel's thirteen. We're on holiday in France.

1 🔊 1.12 Read and listen to Alice's blog. Find Alice in photos A, B and C.

2 Read the blog again. Complete the sentences with one word in each gap.
1 Isabel is Alice's *sister*.
2 Tommy is Isabel's _____.
3 Granny is Alice's dad's _____.
4 Granny's _____ is in London.

3 Read the sentences. Mark them T (true) or F (false).
1 Alice is eleven in photo C.   T / F
2 They're on holiday in France in photo A.   T / F
3 They're in the park in photo B.   T / F
4 Tommy is eleven in photo B.   T / F
5 Photo A is Alice's favourite.   T / F

4 🔊 1.13 Listen and repeat.

VOCABULARY	Places
at home	at school
in the park	on holiday

5 Look at the pictures and write the places.

1 *in the park*   2 _____

3 _____   4 _____

6 Work in pairs. Go to page 140. Take turns describing the photos.

1.6 Listening and Writing
Best friends

INTERNATIONAL FRIENDSHIP DAY!

🏠 Podcasts 🎵 Kids 👥 International Friendship

We think about our friends on International Friendship Day.

Listen to our podcast with your friends!

1 Look at the website. What is the podcast about?

2 🔊 1.14 Listen to the podcast. Match speakers 1–3 with photos of their best friends A–C.

1 Tom _____   2 Maria _____   3 Juan _____

A

B

C

3 🔊 1.14 Read the questions. Listen again. Write a number or a country.
1 How old is Monica? *11*
2 Where is Monica now? _____
3 How old is Shu? _____
4 Where are Ayla and Yusuf from? _____

4 Who is your best friend? Tell the class.

5 Read about Alex and complete the table.

My best friend

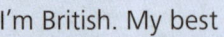

My name's Alex. I'm twelve and I'm from the UK. I'm British. My best friend is Lian. She's twelve too. Lian is from the UK. Lian's dad is British. Lian's mum and granny are Chinese.

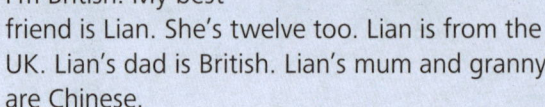

	Name	Age	Nationality	Country
Me	*Alex*			*the UK*
My best friend			*British*	

6 Study the Writing box. Then find the capital letters in the text in Exercise 5.

WRITING — Capital letters

Use a capital letter for names of people, countries and nationalities. Use a capital letter for the pronoun *I* and at the beginning of every sentence too.
My best friend is **J**ack.
I'm from **F**rance.
Maria and **J**uan are **S**panish.

WRITING TIME

7 Write about you and your best friend.

1 Find ideas
Find a photo of you and your best friend.

2 Draft
Write about your name, age, country and nationality.
My name's …
I'm (ten/eleven/twelve …).
I'm from …
Write about your best friend's name, age, country and nationality.

3 Check and write
Check all the capital letters and write the final version of your text.

1.7 CLIL: Art
Families in Art

1 🔊 1.15 Listen and repeat.

VOCABULARY	Art
artist by children painting people picture	

2 In pairs, talk about a family photo. Who is in it?

3 Look at the painting above and read the text. Write the names of the people in the line drawing.

The Copley family
By John Singleton Copley (1738–1815)

This is a painting of the artist's family. The people in the picture are John Singleton Copley; Mrs Copley; Mrs Copley's father, Richard Clarke; the Copleys' three daughters, Betsy (six), Mary (three) Susanna (baby), and son, John Junior (four).

4 Read the text again. Complete the sentences with one word in each gap.
1 John Singleton Copley is the children's *father*.
2 Richard Clarke is the children's _____.
3 Mrs Copley is the children's _____.
4 Betsy is Mary and Susanna's _____.
5 John Junior is the girls' _____.

5 Look at paintings A–C. What is the nationality of the artists?

🇫🇷 by Edgar Degas

🇬🇧 by John Everett Millais   🇫🇷 by Paul Cézanne

6 Match the paintings A–C in Exercise 5 with their titles 1–3.
1 ☐ The artist's father
2 ☐ Portrait of the artist's uncle Henri and his cousin, Lucie
3 ☐ Portrait of Mrs William Evamy (the artist's aunt)

7 Work in pairs. Test your memory. Cover Exercises 5 and 6. Then take turns to make sentences and say if they are correct or incorrect.
1 John Everett Millais / American
2 Paul Cézanne / French
3 Edgar Degas / British
4 Mrs Evamy / Millais' mother
5 Lucie / Degas' cousin
6 Henri / Degas' father

A: *John Everett Millais is American.*
B: *No. He's British.*

B: *Paul Cézanne is French.*
A: *Yes. That's right.*

8 Have a class vote about the paintings in this lesson. Which one do you like best?

I can talk about families in art.

Vocabulary Activator

WORDLIST 🔊 1.16

Family
aunt (n)
brother (n)
cousin (n)
dad (n)
daughter (n)
father (n)
grandad (n)
grandfather (n)
grandmother (n)
granny (n)
mother (n)
mum (n)
parents (n)
sister (n)
son (n)
uncle (n)

Countries and nationalities
American (adj)
British (adj)
China (n)
Chinese (adj)
France (n)
French (adj)
Poland (n)
Polish (adj)
Spain (n)
Spanish (adj)
Turkey (n)
Turkish (adj)
the UK (n)
the USA (n)

Places
at home
at school
in the park
on holiday

Art
artist (n)
by (prep)
children (singular: child) (n)
painting (n)
people (singular: person) (n)
picture (n)

Extra words
Be careful!
best friend
birthday (n)
box (n)
cake (n)

card (n)
classmate (n)
fat (adj)
flag (n)
hamster (n)
happy (adj)
Hold this, please.
holiday (n)
home (n)
I've got it!
Let's have a break.
mouse (n)
neighbour (n)
Nice to meet you.
orange (adj)
portrait (n)
present (n)

1 Complete the puzzle with the family words in the wordlist.

2 What nationality are they? Where are they from?

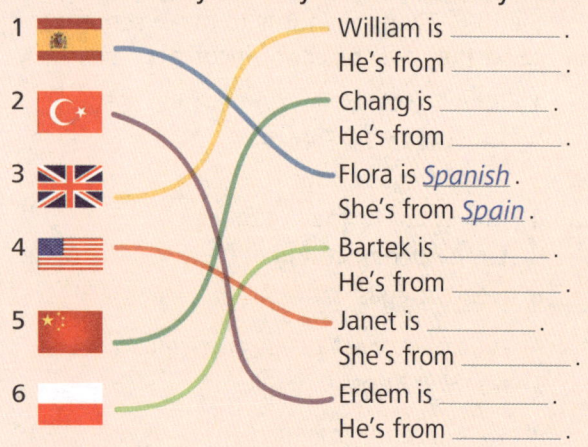

1 William is _____. He's from _____.
2 Chang is _____. He's from _____.
3 Flora is *Spanish*. She's from *Spain*.
4 Bartek is _____. He's from _____.
5 Janet is _____. She's from _____.
6 Erdem is _____. He's from _____.

3 Find words from the wordlist.
1 words that go with *birthday* cake, *card*, _____
2 words that go with *country* nationality, _____
3 groups of people neighbours, _____, family

4 🔊 1.17 **PRONUNCIATION** /v/ or /b/
Listen and repeat.
Viv's **b**est friends,
Vincent and **B**rad,
Are a **b**ad **b**rown dog
And a **v**ery **b**ig cat!

Unit 1 22

Revision

Vocabulary

1 Complete the family words.
1 g _r_ and _a_ d
2 gr _ n _ y
3 un _ _ e
4 a _ _ t
5 m _ m
6 d _ d
7 co _ _ in
8 s _ st _ r
9 b _ _ t _ er

2 Choose the odd one out.
1 ⓐ Chinese   b Spain   c the UK
2 a the USA   b Turkish   c the UK
3 a France   b Poland   c American
4 a Spanish   b British   c China
5 a French   b the USA   c Polish

3 Look at the photos. Choose the correct option.

1 in the park / at school

2 on holiday / in the park

3 at school / on holiday

4 at school / at home

Grammar

4 Complete the sentences. Use possessive 's.
1 Luke / cake   It's _Luke's cake_.
2 Granny / birthday   It's _____.
3 Dad / sister   Megan is _____.
4 Jen / brother   Alex is _____.

5 Read and complete Maria's profile with *am*, *are* or *is*.

My name is Maria. I ¹ _am_ thirteen. I ² _____ from the USA. My best friend ³ _____ Isabel. Isabel ⁴ _____ British. We ⁵ _____ classmates. Isabel's two brothers ⁶ _____ my friends too.

6 Match 1–5 with a–e.
1 ☐ Jane's best
2 ☐ Your brother is
3 ☐ It's my
4 ☐ That isn't
5 ☐ My cousin

a your schoolbag.
b George is eleven.
c friend is Spanish.
d in my class.
e birthday today!

7 Write negative sentences. Which sentences are true for you? Tell your partner.
1 I'm fifteen.
   I'm not fifteen.
2 My best friend is Spanish.
   _____
3 My brother's name is Ben.
   _____
4 We're at home.
   _____
5 It's my birthday.
   _____
6 My neighbours are Chinese.
   _____

Speaking

8 Complete the dialogue with the words below. Then act out the dialogue in groups of three.

> meet   nice   ~~this~~   this

Jamie: Mum, ¹ _this_ is my friend, David. David, ² _____ is my mum.
David: Hello, Mrs Smith. ³ _____ to meet you.
Mum: Nice to ⁴ _____ you too, David.

23 Unit 1

BBC CULTURE
English around the world

Map with labels:
1. ___
2. Canada
3. Ireland
4. ___
5. South Africa
6. ___
7. New Zealand

WHO SPEAKS ENGLISH?

The UK (United Kingdom): England, Wales, Scotland and Northern Ireland
Capital city: London
Population: 65 million people
Language: English

The USA (United States of America)
Capital city: Washington
Population: 324 million people
Language: English and Spanish

Australia
Capital city: Canberra
Population: 24 million people
Language: English

---

capital city (n) an important city where the government of a country, state, etc. is
flag (n) a piece of cloth with a design on it that represents a country
population (n) the number of people living in a country

---

1 Look at the map. Match countries 1, 4 and 6 with the words below.

> Australia   the UK   the USA

2 🔊 1.18 People in the UK, the USA and Australia speak the same language. What language is it? Read, listen and check.

3 Look at the map and read the text again. Read 1–5 and follow the instructions.

1 Choose the Australian flag.
  a 🇬🇧   b 🇺🇸   c 🇦🇺

2 Complete the sentence:
  Scotland is in _____.

3 Number the countries from 1 to 3 (very big, big, small number of people).
  ☐ the UK   ☐ the USA   ☐ Australia

4 Choose the correct option.
  Canberra is in *Australia* / *the USA*.

5 Draw lines and make sentences.
  Ireland   is in the UK.
  Northern Ireland   is a country.

4 🔊 1.19 Listen and match 1–3 with a–c.
1 Erin   a is from the USA.
2 Peter   b is from Australia.
3 Ollie   c is from the UK.

 **This is the UK**

5 ▶ 7 Watch the video and answer the presenter's questions.

6 ▶ 7 Watch the video again. Choose the correct answer.
1. The UK is the United Kingdom of Great Britain and
   a Scotland. b Wales. c Northern Ireland.
2. There are four … in the UK.
   a cities. b countries. c towns.
3. People from the UK are …
   a British. b English. c American.
4. London is a … city.
   a small and busy b big and green
   c big and busy

7 Discuss in class. What new things did you learn from the video? Would you like to visit the UK? Why?/Why not?

PROJECT TIME

8 In groups, make a digital presentation about one of the countries below. Follow these steps.

> the Republic of Ireland   New Zealand   the Republic of South Africa   Canada

 In your group, collect information about the country. Answer these questions.
- What is the capital city?
- What is the population?
- What is the language? / What are the languages?

 Find these things.
- a map of the country
- the flag of the country
- photos of important and/or interesting places

3 Create your presentation.
- Write your presentation.
- Choose the photos to add to your presentation.
- Read and check your presentation.

4 Share your presentation with the class.
- Answer other students' questions.
- Ask questions and comment on the other presentations.

My things

2

VOCABULARY
Clothes | Adjectives | My things | Shapes

GRAMMAR
this, that, these, those | too big/small | to be questions and short answers

2.1 Vocabulary

Clothes

1 Find the clothes below in the picture. Which clothes are you wearing today?

> coat   jeans   shoes   skirt   T-shirt   trousers

2 🔊 **2.1** Listen and repeat. Find the clothes in the Vocabulary box in the picture on page 26.

> **VOCABULARY** — **Clothes**
>
> cap   coat   dress   jacket   jeans   shoes   skirt
> T-shirt   top   tracksuit   trainers   trousers

3 🔊 **2.2** Listen and choose the word you hear.
1 (T-shirt) / skirt
2 jacket / jeans
3 trainers / trousers
4 shoes / dress
5 cap / coat
6 top / tracksuit

> **WATCH OUT!**
> The T-shirt **is** blue.
> The shoes **are** black.
> The jeans **are** blue.

4 Complete the table with the words in the Vocabulary box.

Singular: is	Plural: are
T-shirt, _____,	jeans, _____,
_____, _____,	_____, _____,
_____, _____,	

5 Complete the sentences with *is* or *are*. Then look at the picture on page 26. Tick (✓) for *yes* or put a cross (✗) for *no*.
1 ✓ The tracksuit *is* brown.
2 ☐ The trainers _____ red.
3 ☐ The dress _____ yellow.
4 ☐ The trousers _____ black.

6 Look at your clothes and tell a partner.
My jeans are blue, my T-shirt is green and white, and my trainers are red.

7 Choose a student from your class and name his/her clothes. Ask your partner to guess the student.
A: *White T-shirt, blue skirt.*
B: *It's Natasha!*

8 Adam and Adele are in the gym. Are their clothes OK for the gym? Write their clothes. Then tick (✓) for *yes* or put a cross (✗) for *no*.

Adam: ☐ tracksuit trousers   Adele: ☐ _____
      ☐ jacket   ☐ _____
      ☐ _____   ☐ _____
      ☐ _____   ☐ _____

9 Dress Adam and Adele for a party. Write two lists of clothes. In pairs, compare your lists.
Adam: *white T-shirt, …*
Adele: *blue shoes, …*

YOUR WORLD

10 Make lists of clothes you wear at school and at the weekend.

at school	at the weekend

I can talk about clothes.

2.2 Grammar
this, that, these, those

VIDEO — THAT'S MY T-SHIRT!

Mum: Jen, put these clothes away, please.
Jen: OK, Mum.
Oh, hi! What's up? … What? No!

Ten minutes later …

Jen: Bye, Holly! … Hang on, what are these? These aren't my jeans. They're too long! These are Mum's jeans. Yep … and this is Mum's top.

Mum: Jen, these are your jeans. They're too small for me!
Jen: Oops! Sorry, Mum!
Mum: And that's my top over there.
Jen: Yes, it is. Here you are!

Alex: Jen … Jen, where's my new T-shirt?
Jen: It's over there with your old T-shirts?
Alex: No, those are Dad's T-shirts.
Jen: Oh, then your T-shirt is …

1. ▶ 8 ◀) 2.3 Watch the video. Then listen and read. Are the clothes in the right place?

2. Look at the photos and read the story again. Whose clothes are they? Choose the correct option.
   1 Photo 2: The jeans are *Jen's* / (*Mum's*).
   2 Photo 3: The jeans are *Jen's* / *Mum's*.
   3 Photo 3: The top is *Jen's* / *Mum's*.
   4 Photo 4: The T-shirts are *Dad's* / *Alex's*.

3. ◀) 2.4 Listen and repeat. Find these expressions in the story.

SOUNDS GOOD! What's up? • Hang on. • Here you are. • Over there.

4. Who has got Alex's new T-shirt? Have a class vote. Choose the correct answer.
   a Mum   b Dad   c Jen

5. ▶ 9 ◀) 2.5 Now watch or listen and check.

6 Study the Grammar box. Then watch.

GRAMMAR — *this, that, these, those*

This is Jen's top. This top is Jen's.	That is Alex's T-shirt. That T-shirt is Alex's.
These are Jen's trainers. These trainers are Jen's. 	Those are Alex's trainers. Those trainers are Alex's. 

VIDEO ▶ 10 GET GRAMMAR!

"These aren't my trainers."

"This isn't my T-shirt!"

7 Choose the correct option.
1 *This / (These)* are your trainers.
2 *This / These* isn't Alex's T-shirt.
3 *This / These* shoes aren't Jen's.
4 *That / Those* T-shirts are Dad's.
5 *That / Those* is my coat.
6 *That / Those* jeans are Mum's.

8 Complete the sentences with *this, that, these* or *those*.
1 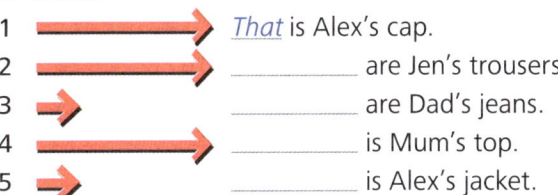 _That_ is Alex's cap.
2 _____ are Jen's trousers.
3 _____ are Dad's jeans.
4 _____ is Mum's top.
5 _____ is Alex's jacket.

9 🔊 2.6 Listen and repeat.

VOCABULARY — Adjectives

big   boring   cool   long   new   old   short   small

10 Look at the words from the Vocabulary box. Match them with their opposites.
1 big   a old
2 boring   b short
3 new   c small
4 long   d cool

11 In pairs, talk about the clothes. Use adjectives from the Vocabulary box and *this, that, these* or *those*.

A: How about the T-shirts?
B: This T-shirt is cool. That T-shirt is boring.

WATCH OUT!
These shoes are **too** big!
This T-shirt is **too** small!

YOUR WORLD

12 Play a drawing dictation game! Use adjectives with *too*.
Draw a boy. The boy's T-shirt is too small. …

I can use *this, that, these, those* and adjectives.   **29** Unit 2

2.3 Grammar
to be questions and short answers

The Terrific Two – Dug's new suit

1. Girl: Are they OK?
Superdug: Yes, they are.
Girl: Thank you!
Boy: Is he a superhero?
Kit: Yes, he is. He's Superdug!

2. Kit: Dug! Your suit is too small!

3. Dug: This suit is cool! Size M? No. Size XL!
Kit: Are you sure, Dug?
Dug: Yes, I am.
Kit: XL is too big for you.
Dug: No, I'm a superhero! I'm big!

4. Two days later …
Kit: Thank you.
Dug: Is this box for me?
Kit: Yes, it is. What is it?
Dug: It's my new suit!

5. Dug: Ready! Am I cool in this suit?
Kit: No, you aren't. The suit is too big! Hmm … Hang on!

6. Dug: Fantastic! You're a clever cat, Kit!

1 Look at the cartoon. Where does Dug buy his superhero suits from?

2 🔊 2.7 Listen and read. What size is Dug's new suit?

Unit 2 30

3 Study the Grammar box. Then watch.

GRAMMAR	to be questions and short answers
?	Short answers
Am I OK?	Yes, I am. / No, I'm not.
Are you OK?	Yes, you are. / No, you aren't.
Is he/she/it OK?	Yes, he/she/it is. / No, he/she/it isn't.
Are we OK?	Yes, we are. / No, we aren't.
Are you OK?	Yes, you are. / No, you aren't.
Are they OK?	Yes, they are. / No, they aren't.
What is it?	It's my new suit.

VIDEO ▶ 11 GET GRAMMAR!

4 Read the sentences. Mark them T (true) or F (false).
1 The puppies are OK.   T / F
2 The girl is a superhero.   T / F
3 Dug's new suit is in the box.   T / F
4 Dug's new suit is small.   T / F

5 Find the questions in the cartoon on page 30. Complete the questions.
1 *Are* they OK?
2 Is _____ a superhero?
3 _____ you sure?
4 _____ this box for me?
5 What is _____?
6 Am _____ cool?

6 Look at the cartoon on page 30. In your notebook, answer the questions in Exercise 5.
1 *Yes, they are.*

7 Complete the questions and short answers.
1 Boy: *Are* you a superhero?
   Kit: No, I*'m not*.
2 Kit: _____ we best friends?
   Dug: Yes, we _____.
3 Dug: _____ my new suit cool?
   Kit: No, it _____.
4 Kit: _____ I clever?
   Dug: Yes, you _____.
5 Girl: _____ Superdug your brother?
   Kit: No, he _____.
6 Kit: _____ they your puppies?
   Girl: Yes, they _____.

8 🔊 2.8 Listen to the questions and choose the correct answer.
1 (Yes, it is) / No, they aren't.
2 Yes, you are. / No, they aren't.
3 Yes, I am. / No, you aren't.
4 Yes, they are. / No, he isn't.
5 Yes, they are. / No, you aren't.
6 Yes, we are. / No, they aren't.

9 Write questions in your notebook. In pairs, ask the questions and give true answers.
1 you / twelve years old?
   Are you twelve years old?
2 you / happy?
3 we / friends?
4 Superdug and Kit / cool?
5 you / clever?
6 I / a superhero?
A: *Are you twelve years old?*
B: *Yes, I am. / No, I'm not.*

YOUR WORLD

10 🔊 2.9 🔊 2.10 Go to page 140. Listen and chant Kit's Rap.

I can ask and answer questions with the verb *to be*.

2.4 Speaking
Asking for personal information

VIDEO ▶ WHAT'S YOUR NAME?

Mr Wood: What's your name?
Lucas: Lucas Ortiz. That's O-R-T-I-Z.
Mr Wood: Good. And how old are you, Lucas?
Lucas: I'm eleven years old.
Mr Wood: Welcome to the school band.

Lian: Where are you from, Lucas?
Lucas: I'm from Madrid, Spain.
Lian: What's your favourite music?
Lucas: Good question. Rock, I think.
Lian: Who's your favourite singer?
Lucas: Erm … Ed Sheeran.
Lian: High five! He's my favourite too!

1 ▶ 12 🔊 2.11 Watch the video. Then listen and read. Where is Lucas from?

2 🔊 2.12 Listen and repeat.

> **SPEAKING** — Asking for personal information
> What's your name?
> How old are you?
> Where are you from?
> What's your favourite *music/sport/film*?
> Who's your favourite *actor/singer/sportsperson*?

3 🔊 2.13 Listen to the short dialogues. Choose the correct option.
1 *Star Wars.* / (*Superman.*)
2 Nick Carr. That's C-A-double R. / Carl Neal. That's N-E-A-L.
3 Portsmouth, UK. / Paris, France.
4 I'm twelve. / I'm thirteen.
5 Ariana Grande. / Taylor Swift.

4 Complete the dialogues with questions from the Speaking box.
1 A: *What's your favourite music*?
   B: Pop, I think.
2 A: _____?
   B: I'm twelve years old.
3 A: _____?
   B: My name's Fred Allen. That's A- double L-E-N.
4 A: _____?
   B: Football.
5 A: _____?
   B: I'm from Glasgow, Scotland.

YOUR WORLD

5 In pairs, ask and answer the questions from the Speaking box. Give crazy answers!
A: What's your name?
B: My name's Queen Coco!
A: Where are you from?
B: I'm from Chocolateland.

I can ask for and give personal information.

2.5 Reading and Vocabulary

My things

1 🔊 2.14 Listen and repeat. Then match photos 1–4 with the words in the Vocabulary box.

VOCABULARY — My things

backpack   laptop computer   mobile phone
mountain bike

1 ....

2 ....

3 ....

4 ....

2 🔊 2.15 Read and listen to the article. Why is the backpack a super backpack?

3 Read the sentences. Mark them T (true) or F (false).
1 Shen is from London in the UK.   T / F
2 The super backpack is a jacket too.   T / F
3 The super backpack is too small for a laptop computer.   T / F
4 Tilly is a cat.   T / F

4 Look at the picture in the article and answer the questions.
1 What colour is the super backpack?
2 Is the jacket red or blue? ....
3 Is the cat big or small? ....

5 Work in groups. Invent a supergadget! Draw it and show it to the class.
This isn't a boring schoolbag. It's a laptop too!

Shen Taylor is 12.
He's from Liverpool in the UK.
Shen's super backpack is our gadget of the week. Why? Read on.

SHEN'S SUPER BACKPACK!

This is my super backpack! It's very, very cool. My super backpack is also a mountain bike. It's small, but it isn't too small. It's fantastic! And that's not all. If I'm cold and my jacket is at home, no problem. This super backpack is a big jacket too.

My super backpack is just right for my laptop computer, my mobile phone and even my cat, Tilly – and she's big! How cool is that!

I can understand a short text about a gadget.

2.6 Listening and Writing
My favourite things

1 In pairs, name the clothes of the people in the picture in Exercise 2. What objects have they got?

2 🔊 2.16 Look at the picture again. Listen and write numbers next to the four names. There is one extra child in the picture.

Sam ☐ Monica ☐ Janet ☐ Ben ☐

3 🔊 2.16 Listen again. Mark the sentences T (true) or F (false).
1 Sam's cap is too small.   T / F
2 Janet is Monica's sister.   T / F
3 Janet's favourite thing is a skateboard. T / F
4 Ben's trainers are red.   T / F
5 Monica's skirt is too short.   T / F

4 What are your favourite things? Tell a friend.

5 Read Alex's blog post. What are his favourite things?

What are my favourite things?

My number one favourite thing is my old, blue mountain bike. I love my bike! My new comic book is number two. It's fantastic! What's number three? That's easy. My red and white trainers. They're really cool!

What are your favourite things? Write a post and tell me.

6 Study the Writing box. Then find the punctuation marks in Alex's blog post.

> **WRITING** Punctuation
>
> Remember to use punctuation marks!
> What are your favourite things**?**
> They're my backpack**,** my phone and my computer.
> They're cool**!**

WRITING TIME

7 Write about your favourite things.

Find ideas
Make a list of your favourite things. Think of adjectives to describe them.

Draft
Write about your favourite things.
Give your text a title: *What are my favourite things?*
My number one/two/three favourite thing is my … It's …

Check and write
Check your punctuation and write the final version of your text.

Unit 2 34 I can understand and write short texts about favourite things.

2.7 CLIL: Geometry
Shapes

1 🔊 **2.17** Listen and repeat. Match pictures 1–5 with the words in the Vocabulary box.

VOCABULARY — Shapes

circle ☐   line ☐   rectangle ☐   square ☐
triangle ☐

1 ～   2 ●   3 ■   4 ▲
5 ▬

2 Read and match texts 1–3 with pictures A–D. There is one extra picture.

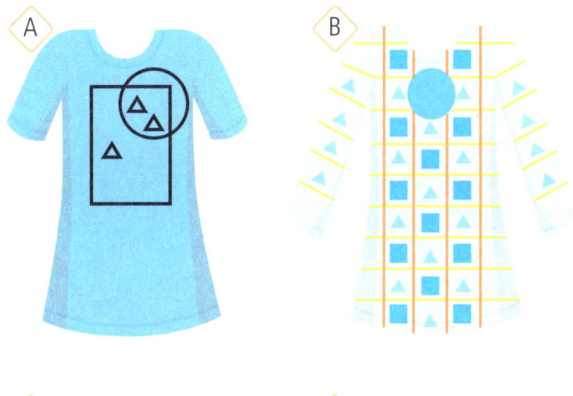

1 ☐ Look! This is my new top. It's cool. It's white with blue squares and triangles and orange and yellow lines. Oh, and a blue circle too.

2 ☐ My favourite top is old, but it isn't boring. It's yellow with red squares, green lines and triangles. No rectangles and no circles!

3 ☐ My favourite top is blue with one big rectangle, small triangles and a circle. No squares or lines!

3 Read the texts and look at the pictures in Exercise 2 again. Complete the table.

Top	Colours	Shapes
A	blue, black	rectangle, triangles, circle
B		
C		

4 Read the sentences. Mark them T (true) or F (false).
1 The rectangle on top A is small.   T / F
2 The shapes on top A are all big.   T / F
3 Top C is yellow with eight squares and eight triangles.   T / F
4 The squares on top C are green.   T / F
5 The circle on top B is blue.   T / F
6 The lines on top B are black and blue.   T / F

5 Design a T-shirt or a top with shapes. Then complete the sentences.

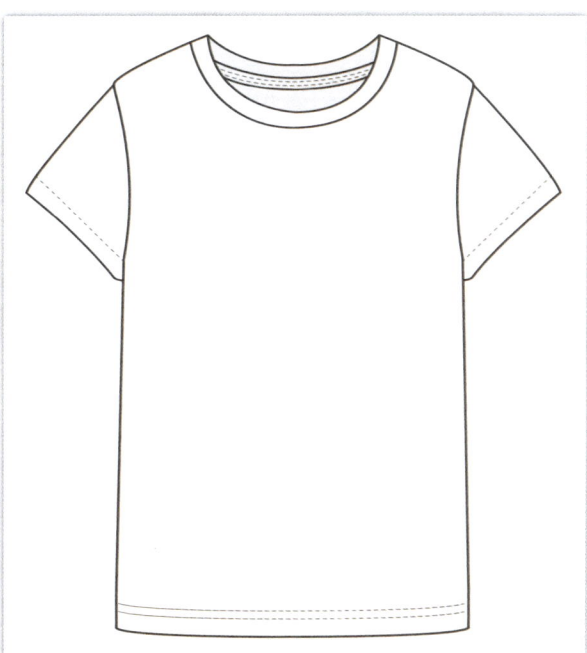

This is my _____ .

It's (colour) _____ with (colours and/or shapes) _____

_____ .

I can describe different shapes.   **35** Unit 2

Vocabulary Activator

WORDLIST 🔊 2.18

Clothes
cap (n)
coat (n)
dress (n)
jacket (n)
jeans (n)
shoes (n)
skirt (n)
T-shirt (n)
top (n)
tracksuit (n)
tracksuit jacket (n)
tracksuit trousers (n)
trainers (n)
trousers (n)

Adjectives
big (adj)
boring (adj)
cool (adj)
long (adj)
new (adj)
old (adj)
short (adj)
small (adj)

My things
backpack (n)
laptop computer (n)
mobile phone (n)
mountain bike (n)

Shapes
circle (n)
line (n)
rectangle (n)
square (n)
triangle (n)

Extra words
Are you sure?
at the weekend
box (n)
boy (n)
clever cat
cold (adj)
fantastic (adj)
favourite (adj)
gadget (n)
girl (n)
Good question.
Hang on.
Here you are.
High five!
How cool is that!
just right

No problem.
Over there.
put away (v)
rock (music) (n)
school band (n)
size (n)
skateboard (n)
suit (n)
That's easy.
That's not all.
too (small) (adv)
What's up?

1 Find words for clothes in the wordlist. Use each word only once.

1 two things for your
   shoes, …

2 three things for   only.

3 one thing for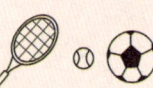

4 two things for when it's

5 one thing for your

6 three things for  and

2 Rewrite the sentences. Use a word that means the opposite of the word in bold.

   cool   old   short   small

1 Your T-shirt is **big**.
   Your T-shirt isn't _____.

2 These trousers aren't **long**.
   _____

3 My tracksuit is **new**.
   _____

4 Those trainers are **boring**.
   _____

3 Complete the words.
My favourite things!
1 My m __ __ i __ e ph __ __ e
2 My m __ u __ __ ai __ b __ k __
3 My l __ p __ op c __ mp __ __ er
4 My new __ __ ck __ ack

4 🔊 2.19 **PRONUNCIATION** /ð/ or /d/
Listen and repeat.
This ol**d** T-shirt is my bro**th**er **D**an's.
That new **d**ress is my mo**th**er Anne's.

Unit 2 36

Revision

Vocabulary

1 Look at the pictures and complete the words. In pairs, say four more clothes words.

Maggie   Diego

1 shoe _s_
2 co __ t
3 t __ p
4 ca __
5 tr __ i __ e __ s
6 je __ __ s
7 T- sh __ __ t
8 ja __ __ __ t

2 Match pictures A–C with sentences 1–2. In pairs, describe the extra picture.

1 ☐ It's old, but it isn't boring. It's green.
2 ☐ It's new. It isn't small and it isn't big. It's red. It's cool!

3 Find and write four objects.

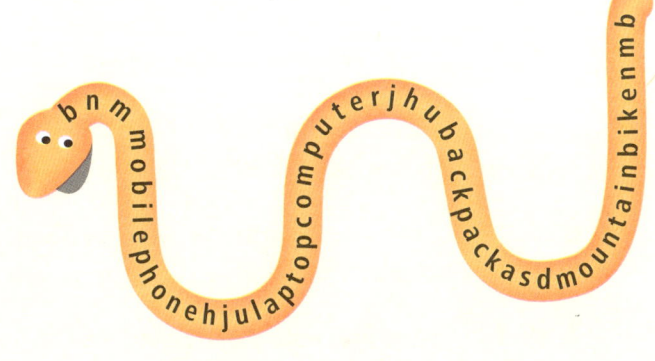

_____, _____, _____, _____

4 In pairs, play a game.
Student A, say an adjective and a clothes word.
  A cool T-shirt!
Student B, say an adjective and a different clothes word.
  New trousers!
Continue! You can't repeat the clothes words. You can repeat the adjectives.

Grammar

5 Look at the pictures in Exercise 1 again. In pairs, say sentences with *too*.
Maggie's coat is too big.

6 Match 1–5 with a–e.
1 These are my favourite
2 Those trousers
3 Those aren't
4 That phone is
5 This is my old

a old and boring.
b Nick and Timmy's backpacks.
c brown bike.
d trainers.
e are too long.

7 Write questions in your notebook. Answer *yes* (✓) or *no* (✗). Use short answers.
1 your backpack / blue? ✓
   Is your backpack blue? Yes, it is.
2 those / your books?   ✗
3 he / at school?   ✓
4 she / Italian?   ✗
5 you / my best friend? ✓

Speaking

8 Complete the questions. Then work in pairs. Student A, you are your favourite star. Student B, ask Student A questions 1–5. Then change roles and have the conversation again.
1 *What's* your name?
2 How old _____ you?
3 Where are _____ from?
4 What _____ your favourite music?
5 _____'s your favourite actor?

SET FOR LIFE

Great idea!

1 Look at the photo. What is the situation?

2 Match expressions 1–4 with photos A–B.

A

B

1 ☐ That's an awful idea!
2 ☐ That's a great idea!
3 ☐ I like it!
4 ☐ I hate it!

3 It is your friend's birthday. You and another friend want to buy him/her a present together. In pairs, make suggestions. Add one suggestion of your own.

> How about a green T-shirt?

> That's a great idea! I like it!

1 a red tracksuit?
2 orange and brown trousers?
3 a superhero suit?
4 a toy car?
5 a painting of a cat?

4 🔊 2.20 Abbie, Brian and Chris are talking about their friend Lucy's birthday. Listen and choose the correct option.
1 When is Lucy's birthday? *Friday* / *today*
2 What kind of restaurant is it? a *pizza* / *Chinese* restaurant

5 🔊 2.21 Listen. Which is a good answer, a or b? Why?
a Ugh! That's an awful idea!
b I'm not sure. How about Chinese?

6 🔊 2.22 Listen and choose the correct option.
Lucy likes *pizza* / *Chinese food*.

7 🔊 2.23 Listen and vote for the best way to finish the dialogue.
a No, I hate pizza! I want Chinese!
b Well, OK. It's Lucy's day, and you all like pizza.

Units 1–2 38 I can make decisions when I am working in a group.

Make decisions as a group

8 🔊 2.24 Read the Useful Tips. Then listen to the friends again. Is Chris doing what the tips say?

9 Complete the dialogues. Dialogue 1 is about a film and dialogue 2 is about a concert. Use expressions from the Useful Phrases box. Then act out the dialogues in groups of three.

1 A: How about *My Fantastic Friend*?
   B: _____
   C: But we all like the actors.
   A: And it's a new film.
   B: _____

2 A: _____
   B: I'm not sure. She isn't my favourite singer. How about the Ed Sheeran concert?
   A: _____
   C: And it's our favourite type of music.
   B: Well, OK, then.

SET FOR LIFE

10 Read the Useful Tips and the expressions in the Useful Phrases box again. In groups, plan a special day out for your friend's birthday.

1 Think about the things your friend likes to do.

2 Write your suggestions on a piece of paper. Find the words you need.

3 In your group, discuss your suggestions. Make a decision.

4 Present your plan to the class.

USEFUL TIPS

When you make decisions as a group, listen to the other people in your group. What do they want to do? Accept the group's decision.

People like different things. When you disagree with a suggestion, be polite.

USEFUL PHRASES

- … is good, but ….
- He/She likes/hates …
- How about a(n)/the …?
- I like/hate …
- I'm not sure.
- It's/It isn't my favourite (type of music/film/book).
- That's a great idea!
- We all like/hate …
- Well, OK, then.

Progress Check Units 1–2

Vocabulary and Grammar

1 Look and read. Tick (✓) for *yes* or put a cross (✗) for *no*.

1. ✓ This is a dog.
2. ☐ This is a skirt.
3. ☐ This is the Spanish flag.
4. ☐ These are mountain bikes.
5. ☐ This is a park.
6. ☐ These are jeans.

2 Look at the picture. Then read and complete the text.

Hi, I'm Peter. I'm in ¹<u>the UK</u> now, but my family and I are from ² _____ . My school clothes are this blue ³ _____ , this white ⁴ _____ and ⁵ _____ grey trousers. My favourite clothes are over there. ⁶ _____ 're my blue jeans, my T-shirt and my grey ⁷ _____ . My T-shirt is black with a white ⁸ _____ and red ⁹ _____ .

Speaking

3 Look at the pictures. Match a–h with 1–6. There are two extra sentences.

a Nice to meet you. ____
b Who's your favourite actor? ____
c This is my mum. ____
d Caz, this is Jack. ____
e Hello, Caz! ____
f He's my neighbour. ____
g What's your favourite music? ____
h Nice to meet you too, Mrs Smith. ____

4 In pairs, ask and answer the questions.
1 What are your favourite weekend clothes?
2 What colour is your T-shirt/top today?
3 What's in your schoolbag today? (Don't look!)
4 What's your favourite place?

Listening

5 🔊 2.25 Read the questions. Listen and write a name or a number.

1 What's the man's surname?   *Smith*
2 What's the boy's name?   _____
3 Who's the boy's best friend?   _____
4 How old is the boy?   _____
5 What's the number of the boy's house?   _____

Reading

6 In pairs, say what you can see in the photo.

7 Read the text. Choose the correct title.
  a My new cat
  b Me and my family

> Hi, I'm Cheryl. I'm twelve and my favourite colour is pink. My pink mobile phone is my favourite thing. My clothes are pink too. Milo, my cat, isn't pink! He's brown and white.
>
> My family is very big. My sisters' names are Sarah and Daniela. My brothers' names are Rob and Mick. My dad is an actor. Sometimes he's on TV! My mum is a singer. She's cool. My granny and grandad are from Spain. Are we a happy family? Yes, we are!

8 Read the text in Exercise 7 again. Answer the questions in your notebook.
1 How old is Cheryl?
  Cheryl is twelve.
2 What's Cheryl's favourite thing?
3 Is Cheryl's family small?
4 Who are Rob and Mick?
5 Is Cheryl's mum boring?
6 Where is Cheryl's grandmother from?

Writing

9 Write 40–50 words about you and your family. Use these questions to help you.
1 What's your name?
2 How old are you?
3 What's your favourite colour?
4 What are your favourite things?
5 Where is your family from?
  Hi! My name's …

In the house

3

VOCABULARY
In the house | Prepositions of place |
Household objects | Materials

GRAMMAR
there is/there are
affirmative | *there is/there are* negative and questions

3.1 Vocabulary

In the house

1 Match the household objects 1–8 in the photos with the words below.

bath   bed   chair   desk   door   sofa   table   window

Unit 3   42

2 🔊 **3.1** Listen and repeat. Find the things in the Vocabulary box in the photos on page 42.

> **VOCABULARY** ▸ **In the house**
>
> **Parts of the house**
> bathroom   bedroom   door   floor   garage
> garden   kitchen   living room   wall   window
>
> **Inside the house**
> armchair   bath   bed   chair   desk   fridge
> sofa   table

3 Which part of the house are the photos? Choose the correct option.

1 living room / (bedroom)
2 bathroom / kitchen 
3 garage / bathroom 
4 bedroom / living room 
5 living room / garden 
6 floor / wall 

4 🔊 **3.2** Listen to the sounds. Where are you? Write in your notebook.
  1 *In the living room.*

5 Read the sentences and complete the words.
  1 It's in the bedroom.
     b _e_ d
  2 It's in the kitchen.
     f __ id __ e
  3 It's in the living room.
     a __ __ ch __ ir
  4 It's in the kitchen.
     t __ b __ e
  5 It's in the bedroom.
     d __ __ k
  6 It's in the bathroom.
     b __ t __
  7 It's in the kitchen.
     ch __ __ r
  8 It's in the living room.
     s __ f __

6 In pairs, look at the photos on page 42. Student A, say a sentence about an object inside the house. It can be a true sentence or a false sentence. Student B, is Student A's sentence true or false? Correct the false sentences. Then change roles and have the conversation again.

  A: The armchair is in the bathroom.
  B: No, it isn't. It's in the living room!

YOUR WORLD

7 Draw household objects in your Crazy House. Then make lists and compare in pairs.

The kitchen: a sofa, …

bedroom

bathroom   kitchen

I can talk about my house.   **43**   Unit 3

3.2 Grammar
there is/there are affirmative

VIDEO ▶ THERE'S A PHONE ON THE SOFA!

1

Alex: Jen, where's the orange juice?
Jen: It's in the fridge.
Alex: Where?
Jen: Right there! It's next to the milk.
Alex: Oh, there it is!

2

Alex: Where's my phone?
Lian: There's a phone on the sofa.
Jen: No, that's my phone.
Lian: Is it under the table?
Jen: No, it isn't.

3

Lian: Is it under the sofa?
Alex: No, it isn't, but there are two DVDs.
Jen: Hey! Those are my DVDs!

4

Alex: Wait! There are some sweets under the sofa!
Jen: Yuck! They're old!
Alex: But where's my phone?
Lian: Hang on!

1 ▶ 13 🔊 3.3 Watch the video. Then listen and read. What is Alex looking for? Choose the correct answer.
   a a book   b his phone   c two DVDs

SOUNDS GOOD!   Right there! • There it is!
• Wait! • Yuck!

2 Look at the photos. Answer the questions in your notebook.
  1 Photo 1: Where are the three friends?
    They're in the kitchen.
  2 Photo 2: Where are they now?
  3 Photo 2: Is it Jen's phone?
  4 Photo 3: Are they Alex's DVDs?
  5 Photo 4: What's wrong with the sweets?

3 🔊 3.4 Listen and repeat. Find these expressions in the story.

4 Guess where Alex's phone is. Use *in*, *on* or *under*.

5 ▶ 14 🔊 3.5 Now watch or listen and check.

6 Study the Grammar box. Then watch.

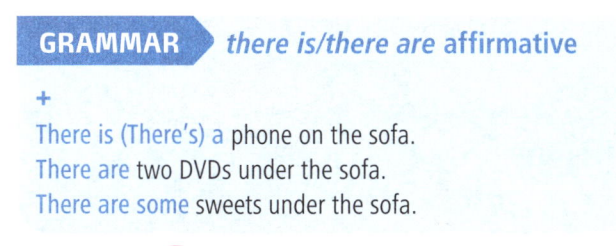

GRAMMAR *there is/there are* affirmative

+
There is (There's) a phone on the sofa.
There are two DVDs under the sofa.
There are some sweets under the sofa.

VIDEO ▶ **15 GET GRAMMAR!**

There are two rats under the table.

There's a rat under the sofa.

7 Complete the sentences with *There is* or *There are*. Then look at the photos on page 44 and tick (✓) the true sentences.
1 Photo 1 ✓ — *There is* a fridge.
2 Photo 1 ☐ — _____ three phones.
3 Photo 2 ☐ — _____ two chairs.
4 Photo 2 ☐ — _____ a table.
5 Photo 3 ☐ — _____ a sofa.
6 Photo 3 ☐ — _____ two doors.

8 Look around you. Say how many of the things below there are in your classroom.

| board   desk   door   girls and boys   teacher |
| wall   window |

There's one door. There are two windows.

9 🔊 3.6 Look, listen and repeat.

VOCABULARY Prepositions of place

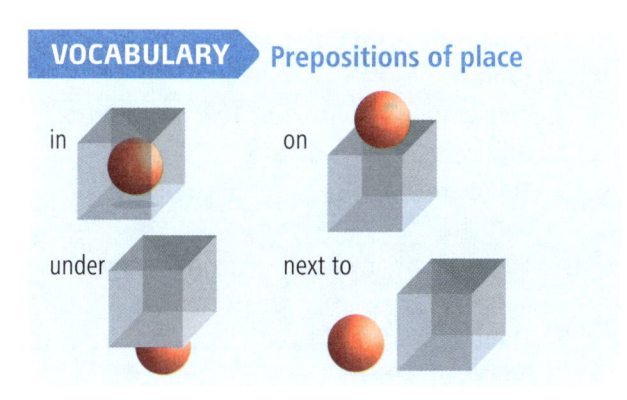

in   on

under   next to

10 Look at the photos on page 44. Choose the correct option.
1 Photo 1: There are two phones *under* / **on** the kitchen table.
2 Photo 1: There is orange juice *in* / *on* the fridge.
3 Photo 1: Lian is *on* / *next to* Jen.
4 Photo 2: There are some books *under* / *next to* the table.

11 Look at pictures A and B. Complete the sentences with prepositions of place.

A

B

1 There's a chair …
 A *next to* the desk.   B _____ the bed.
2 _____ a bag …
 A _____ the door.   B _____ the box.
3 There are some books …
 A _____ the bag.   B _____ the table.
4 _____ some T-shirts …
 A _____ the bed.   B _____ the bed.

YOUR WORLD
12 Go to page 141 and play a drawing dictation game.

I can use *there is/there are* and prepositions of place.   **45**   Unit 3

3.3 Grammar

there is/there are negative and questions

The Terrific Two – Dug and Coco

1 KIT! HELP! THERE ARE TWO BAD PEOPLE HERE!

Kit: Dug! It's my granny! Go to 10 Paxton Street!
Dug: OK.

2
Dug: Kit, there isn't a number on the house.
Kit: Is there a blue car in the garage?
Dug: Yes, there is.
Kit: Are there two big trees?
Dug: Yes, there are.
Kit: That's Granny's house.

3
Dug: Where are the bad people?
Granny: There aren't any bad people here, Dug.
Parrot: Help! Kit! Help!

4
Dug: Kit, it's the parrot, not your granny!
Kit: Coco? Oh, he's naughty!
Granny: I'm very sorry, Dug. Coco is a silly boy!
Parrot: Silly boy, Coco! Sorry, Dug!
Granny: Good boy, Coco!

5 GOOD BOY COCO! SILLY BOY, DUG!

1 Look at the cartoon. How do Kit and Superdug talk when he is in the air? Choose the correct picture.

A B C

2 🔊 3.7 Listen and read. Who says 'Kit! Help!' on the phone? Choose the correct answer.

a Kit's granny   b Coco, the parrot

3 Complete the sentences with words from the cartoon.
1 Kit's granny's *house* is at 10 Paxton Street.
2 Granny's _____ is blue.
3 There are two big _____ in Granny's garden.
4 There aren't any bad _____ in Granny's house.
5 There's only Granny and _____ in the house.

Unit 3   46   I can use the negative and question forms of *there is / there are*.

4 Study the Grammar box. Then watch.

GRAMMAR — *there is/there are* negative and questions

–	There isn't a red car.	There aren't any people.
?	Is there a red car? Yes, there is. / No, there isn't.	Are there any people? Yes, there are. / No, there aren't.

VIDEO ▶ 16 GET GRAMMAR!

Are there any cupcakes?

Yes, there are.

5 Choose the correct option. Then look at the cartoon on page 46 and tick (✓) the true sentences.
1 ✓ *There isn't /* **There aren't** any people in Granny's garden.
2 ☐ *There isn't / There aren't* any cats in the story.
3 ☐ *There isn't / There aren't* a bike in Granny's garage.
4 ☐ *There isn't / There aren't* any dogs in Granny's garden.
5 ☐ *There isn't / There aren't* a phone in Granny's house.
6 ☐ *There isn't / There aren't* a desk in the living room.

⚠ WATCH OUT!
There isn't **a** tree.   Is there **a** tree?
There aren't **any** trees.   Are there **any** trees?

6 Look at the cartoon on page 46. What is missing? Choose from the words below.

door   pictures   table   TV   ~~window~~

1 Picture 1: Look at the wall.
  There isn't a window.
2 Picture 2: Look at Granny's house.
3 Picture 3: Look at the table.
4 Picture 4: Look at the books.
5 Picture 5: Look at the wall.

7 Look at the picture. In your notebook, write Kit's questions and Dug's answers. Then ask and answer the questions in pairs.

1 house with a blue door next to the big house?
  Kit: Is there a house with a blue door next to the big house?
  Dug: Yes, there is.
2 cars next to the houses?
3 dog under the tree?
4 people in the street?
5 table in the garden?
6 armchairs in the garden?

YOUR WORLD
8 Go to page 141 and play a memory game.

I can use the negative and question forms of *there is/there are*.   **47** Unit 3

3.4 Speaking
Having a guest

VIDEO ▶ WHERE'S THE BATHROOM?

1
Jen: Hi! Here are your books.
Lucas: Thanks, Jen. Please come in. Would you like a sandwich?
Jen: Yes, please. I'm really hungry.

2
Jen: This is yummy!
Lucas: Erm … Jen? There's ketchup on your T-shirt.
Jen: Oh, no! Where's the bathroom, please?
Lucas: Let me show you.

3
Lucas: Is your T-shirt OK?
Jen: Not really. But I'd like another sandwich, please!

1 ▶ 17 🔊 3.8 Watch the video. Then listen and read. Whose house is it? Choose the correct answer.
  a Jen's   b Lian's   c Lucas's

2 🔊 3.9 Listen and repeat.

> **SPEAKING** Having a guest
>
> A: Hello. Please come in.
> B: Thank you.
> A: Would you like *a sandwich*?
> B: Yes, please./No, thank you.
> A: Where's the *bathroom*, please?
> B: It's *next to the living room*.
>   Let me show you.

3 Match 1–3 with a–c. Then act out the dialogues in pairs.
  1 ☐ A: Would you like a biscuit?
  2 ☐ A: Where's the kitchen, please?
  3 ☐ A: Where's my jacket, please?

  a   B: Let me show you.
  b   B: It's on the chair, next to the sofa.
  c   B: Yes, please.

4 Choose the best answer.
  1 A: Hello, Maria. Please come in.
    B: a Yes, please.
       b Thank you.
       c Let me show you.
  2 A: Would you like an ice cream?
    B: a Come in.
       b It's in the fridge.
       c Yes, please.
  3 A: Where's the bathroom?
    B: a Please come in.
       b Let me show you.
       c It's next to the bed.

5 Write dialogues. Then act them out in pairs.
  1 A: hi / come in   B: thank
     Hi. Please come in.   *Thank you.*
  2 A: like / a cupcake?   B: no / thank
  3 A: like / an apple?   B: yes
  4 A: where / the bathroom? B: it's / let me show

YOUR WORLD

6 You have a guest from another planet. In pairs, write dialogues. Make them funny or crazy! Then act them out in class.
  A: Hello, Ziggy. Please come in. Would you like a chair?
  B: Yes, please. I'm really hungry!

Unit 3 48 I can ask for something and ask where something is.

3.5 Reading and Vocabulary
A dream house

1 🔊 3.10 Listen and repeat. Then match photos 1–6 with the words in the Vocabulary box.

VOCABULARY › **Household objects**

carpet   cushion   lamp   plant   poster   television (TV)

1 _____   2 _____   3 _____
4 _____   5 _____   6 _____

2 Which objects in Exercise 1 are in your living room? Where are they? Tell a partner.

3 🔊 3.11 Look, read and listen. What is the text about? Choose the correct answer.
   a a sport   b a person   c a house

4 Read the text again and choose *yes*, *no* or *no information*.
   1 People skateboard in the house.
      yes / no / no information
   2 There are posters on the walls.
      yes / no / no information
   3 There's a TV in the living room.
      yes / no / no information
   4 There's a sofa in the house.
      yes / no / no information
   5 There's a carpet in the bedroom.
      yes / no / no information
   6 There's a garage next to the house.
      yes / no / no information

5 Read the text again. Answer the questions.
   1 What rooms are there in the house?
   2 What objects are there in the house?
   3 What objects from the Vocabulary box in Exercise 1 are NOT in the house?

6 Imagine your dream house. Write five sentences about it in your notebook. Tell your partner.

There are … rooms. There's a … and there are … . In my … there's a small/big …

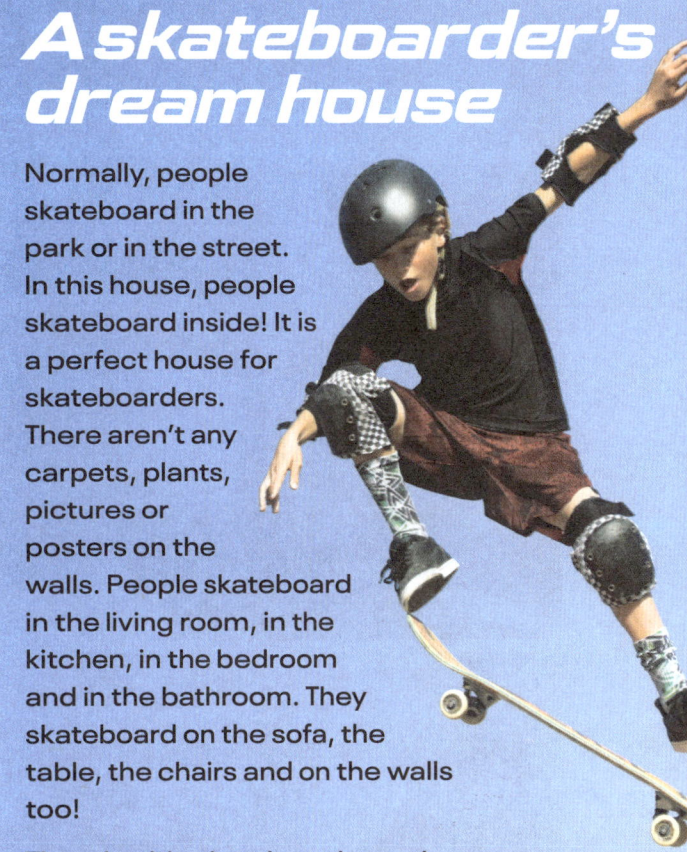

A skateboarder's dream house

Normally, people skateboard in the park or in the street. In this house, people skateboard inside! It is a perfect house for skateboarders. There aren't any carpets, plants, pictures or posters on the walls. People skateboard in the living room, in the kitchen, in the bedroom and in the bathroom. They skateboard on the sofa, the table, the chairs and on the walls too!

There's a big skateboard practice room too. People skateboard with friends and they have competitions there. It's really cool!

I can understand a text about a dream house.

3.6 Listening and Writing
My bedroom

1 Look at photos A–C and find the objects below. Which is your favourite bedroom? Why?

> chair   cushion   desk   plant

A

B

C

2 🔊 3.12 Listen and match speakers 1 and 2 with bedrooms A–C in Exercise 1. There is one extra bedroom.

☐ Speaker 1   ☐ Speaker 2

3 🔊 3.12 Complete the sentences with prepositions of place. Then listen again and check.

Speaker 1
1 My bed is *next to* the window.
2 There's a plant _____ my desk, _____ my laptop.

Speaker 2
3 There are two beds _____ my bedroom.
4 There's a green carpet _____ the floor.

4 Work in pairs. Describe one of the photos in Exercise 1 for your partner to guess.

5 The bedroom in photo A is Lucas's. Read his blog post and complete the sentence.
In Lucas's bedroom there isn't a _____.

LUCAS'S BLOG

My bed is next to the window. There are some cushions on it. Next to my bed, there are two plants and a lamp. There are four boxes on the floor for my things. There's a brown desk and a white chair. There are posters and pictures on the wall. My room is great!

6 Study the Writing box. Then find the apostrophe in Lucas's blog post.

WRITING › Apostrophes

Remember to use apostrophes with short forms.
there **is** = there's   is n**o**t = isn't
are n**o**t = aren't   it **is** = it's
they **a**re = they're   that **is** = that's

7 Add apostrophes to these sentences.
1 There isn't a desk in my bedroom.
2 Theres a plant.
3 Its under the bed.
4 There arent any books.

WRITING TIME

8 Write about your bedroom.

1 Find ideas
Make a list of objects in your bedroom. Write where they are.

2 Draft
Write about your bedroom. Give your text a title.
My bed is …
There's/There isn't a …
There are/There aren't any …

3 Check and write
Check the apostrophes and write the final version of your text.

I can understand and write short texts describing a room.

3.7 CLIL: Science
Materials

1 🔊 3.13 Listen and repeat. Find the materials in photos 1–6 below.

VOCABULARY ▸ Materials

cardboard   glass   metal   paper   wood/wooden

2 Look at the picture. What is 'recycled'?

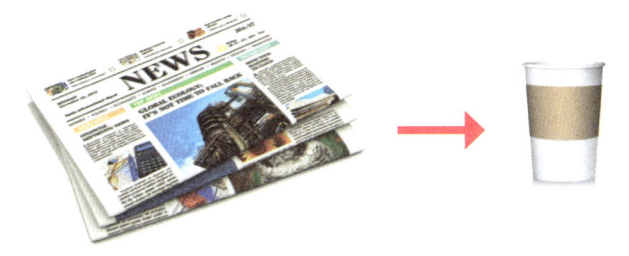

recycled = a new thing from an old thing

3 Match photos 1–6 with a–f.
- a ☐ paper lamp
- b ☐ cardboard chair
- c ☐ metal bath
- d ☐ wooden table
- e ☐ glass window
- f ☐ metal sofa

4 Read the text and look at photos 1–6. Which household object is missing from the text?

5 Read the text again. Mark the questions Y (yes) or N (no).
1. Is the house nice?   Y / N
2. Is the table recycled?   Y / N
3. Is the lamp metal?   Y / N
4. Is the bath old?   Y / N
5. Is the window recycled?   Y / N
6. Is the sofa in the kitchen? Y / N

6 Think of three materials for each object.

Bed	Lamp	Door	Desk

7 What is there in your house? Choose the correct options and complete the sentences.

There's a *cardboard / glass / metal / paper / wooden* _____ in _____ .
There are *some / two cardboard / glass / metal / paper / wooden* _____ in _____ .
They're *great / nice / OK / not nice*.

Is your house eco-friendly?

My house is very nice. There are many recycled household objects in it. This wooden coffee table is in the living room and it's recycled. This paper lamp is in my bedroom. In the bathroom there's this metal bath. It's very old. This beautiful glass window is in the kitchen. The glass is recycled, but it's very old too. My favourite object is the metal sofa in the living room. It's really cool!

I can talk and write about different materials.

Vocabulary Activator

WORDLIST 🔊 3.14

In the house
bathroom (n)
bedroom (n)
door (n)
floor (n)
garage (n)
garden (n)
kitchen (n)
living room (n)
wall (n)
window (n)
armchair (n)
bath (n)
bed (n)
chair (n)
desk (n)
fridge (n)
sofa (n)
table (n)

Prepositions of place
in (prep)
next to (prep)
on (prep)
under (prep)

Household objects
carpet (n)
cushion (n)
lamp (n)
plant (n)
poster (n)
television (TV) (n)

Materials
cardboard (n)
glass (n)
metal (n)
paper (n)
wood/wooden (n, adj)

Extra words
another (determiner)
bad (adj)
car (n)
competition (n)
dream house
DVD (n)
go (v)
I'd like …

inside (adv)
milk (n)
naughty (adj)
Not really.
number (n)
orange juice (n)
parrot (n)
people (n)
perfect (adj)
picture (n)
recycled (adj)
Right here!
silly (adj)
skateboarder (n)

1 Match objects 1–6 with places a–f.
1 fridge
2 bed
3 bath
4 sofa
5 plant
6 car

a bedroom
b garage
c living room
d bathroom
e kitchen
f garden

2 Label the household objects.

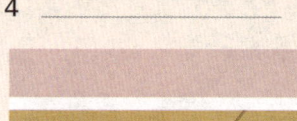

1 _armchair_
2 _____ 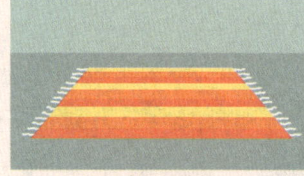 
3 _____  
4 _____ 
5 _____ 
6 _____ 

3 Look at the picture and write sentences. Use prepositions of place.

1 cushion / box
The cushion is in the box.
2 chair / desk
_____
3 lamp / desk
_____
4 poster / wall
_____

4 🔊 3.15 **PRONUNCIATION** /ɪ/ or /iː/
Listen and repeat.
There are sixteen TVs in the living room.
And three big fridges in the kitchen!

Unit 3   52

Revision

Vocabulary

1 Work in pairs. Student A, choose a square. Student B, say where where you can find the object in your house. Then change roles and have the conversation again.

A: 3B
B: Lamp … There's a lamp on my desk.

	1	2	3	4
A	bath	bed	desk	door
B	fridge	sofa	lamp	chair
C	poster	window	table	cushion

2 Read the riddles. Write the objects.
1 There are three on my bedroom wall. p<u>osters</u>
2 It's on the floor in the living room. c_____
3 It's in the living room. There's a film on it now! T_____
4 They're green. They're in my garden. p_____
5 There's one in the living room. I sit in it. a_____

3 Look at the picture. Complete the sentences with prepositions of place.
1 There's a sofa <u>in</u> the living room.
2 There are cushions ____ the beds.
3 There's a plant ____ the sofa.
4 There's a dog ____ the kitchen.
5 The cat is ____ the door.
6 The trainers are ____ the bed.

4 The words for places in the house are mixed up. Write them correctly.
1 kit<u>groom</u>   <u>kitchen</u>
2 bedh<u>room</u>   _____
3 gar<u>room</u>   _____
4 bat<u>rage</u>   _____
5 liv<u>inden</u>   _____
6 gar<u>chen</u>   _____

Grammar

5 Look at the picture in Exercise 3. Complete the text with *there's, there isn't, there are* or *there aren't*.
¹<u>There are</u> five rooms in the house. ²_____ a living room and there's a kitchen. ³_____ a bathroom and ⁴_____ two bedrooms. ⁵_____ a garden, but there's a garage. ⁶_____ any windows in the garage.

6 Write questions about the house in Exercise 3. Use *Is there* or *Are there*.
1 <u>Is there</u> a table in the living room?
2 _____ a TV in the kitchen?
3 _____ any plants in the living room?
4 _____ a dog the kitchen?
5 _____ a lamp in the blue bedroom?
6 _____ any cushions in the bathroom?

7 Look at the picture in Exercise 3 again and answer the questions in Exercise 6 in your notebook.
1 *Yes, there is.*

Speaking

8 Complete the dialogue with the words below.

| come | ~~hi~~ | please | show | where's |
| would | | | | |

Marianna: ¹<u>Hi</u>, Louise. Please ²_____ in!
Louise: Thanks.
Marianna: ³_____ you like a drink?
Louise: Yes, ⁴_____.
Louise: ⁵_____ your room, Marianna?
Marianna: Let me ⁶_____ you.

BBC CULTURE

What do houses look like in the UK?

a detached house

terraced houses

semi-detached houses

a cottage

a houseboat

a flat

a block of flats

1 There are different types of houses in the UK. In pairs, talk about where you can find the houses in the photos.
  a in the city
  b in the country
  c in the city and in the country

2 🔊 3.16 Read the texts and choose the correct option. Then listen and check.

Ian, 11: I live in a *houseboat / semi-detached house*. I am friends with the boys next door. There's a big tree in their garden with a treehouse. We play there all the time!

Lisa, 13: I live in a *block of flats / detached house* with twelve floors. The flat isn't big. There are two small bedrooms, but the living room is nice. The view is fantastic!

Claire, 12: I live in the city, in a street with *terraced houses / cottages*. They are all tall and grey, but the doors are different colours. The door of my house is yellow!

3 🔊 3.17 Listen and complete the texts with the words below.

| boring | cottage | ~~country~~ | houseboat |
| next to | small | | |

Tamsyn, 12: I live in the ¹*country*. My house is a ²_____ in Devon, south England. There are lots of trees ³_____ it.

Matt, 13: I live in a ⁴_____ on the River Thames. It is very ⁵_____, but I like it. The view from my window is never ⁶_____!

fantastic (adj) very attractive
floor (n) one of the levels in a building
view (n) what you can see from somewhere

BBC ▶ Hampton Court Palace

4 ▶ 18 Watch the video and answer the presenter's questions. Then choose the correct answer.
There's a painting of _____ at Hampton Court.
a King Charles
b Queen Elizabeth
c King Henry

5 ▶ 18 Watch the video again. Complete the sentences with one word in each gap.
1 Hampton Court Palace is in _____.
2 There are _____ kings or queens in Hampton Court today.
3 There are over 1,000 _____ in Hampton Court.
4 There is a maze in the _____ of Hampton Court.

6 Discuss in pairs. Which part of Hampton Court Palace is your favourite? Why?

PROJECT TIME

7 In groups, make a digital presentation of interesting or unusual houses all over the world.

1 Individually, find one photo of an interesting or unusual house.
- Look for photos on the internet.

2 Write a description of the house. Find new words you need in a dictionary. Use these questions to help you.
- Where is the house?
- What type of house is it?
- Is it big/small?
- What colour is it?
- Is there a garden/garage? Are there any trees?

3 In your group, put the photos and texts together.

4 Share your presentation with the class.
- Which is your favourite house? Why?

Unusual or interesting houses all over the world
- This house is in …
- It's a (detached) house …
- It's big/small/nice/grey …
- There's/There isn't a (tree) …
- It's unusual/interesting because it's …

About me

4

VOCABULARY
Face, eyes, hair | Parts of the body | Personality adjectives | Adjectives

GRAMMAR
have got affirmative and negative | Regular and irregular plurals | have got questions and short answers | Possessive adjectives

SAM

REGAN

PARK HILL Secondary School

MARIA

ANDY

4.1 Vocabulary

Face, eyes, hair

1 Say the words and point at the features of your face.

ears   eyes   hair   mouth   nose

Unit 4   56

2 🔊 **4.1** Listen and repeat. Which features can you find in the photos on page 56?

> **VOCABULARY** Face, eyes, hair
>
> **Face**
> ears   eyes   mouth   nose
> **Eyes**
> blue   brown   green
> **Hair**
> curly   spiky   straight   wavy
> blond   brown   dark   grey   red

3 Find numbers 1–5 in the photos on page 56. Whose features are they? Complete the sentences.
1 They're *Sam's ears*.
2 It's _____.
3 It's _____.
4 They're _____.
5 It's _____.

4 In pairs, put the words below in the correct list. You can use some words more than once.

> big   blond   blue   brown   curly
> dark   green   grey   long   red
> short   small   spiky   straight   wavy

1	eyes
2	ears / nose / mouth
3	hair

> **WATCH OUT!**
> Maria's hair **is** brown.

5 Look at the photos on page 56. Choose the correct option.
1 Regan's eyes are *brown* / (*green*).
2 Sam's hair is *long* / *short*.
3 Maria's hair is *curly* / *wavy*.
4 Andy's hair is *straight* / *wavy*.
5 Sam's hair is *blond* / *dark*.
6 Regan's hair is *blond* / *red*.
7 Andy's eyes are *blue* / *brown*.

6 Look at the children's hair. Complete the words.

a ☐ str *a i* ght   b ☐ w ___ y

c ☐ _ u _ l _   d ☐ _ _ ik _ _

e ☒ *1* l ___ g   f ☐ _ h _ r _

7 🔊 **4.2** Listen and number the pictures in Exercise 6.
1 Long, straight, red hair, green eyes.
2 Short, curly, brown hair, blue eyes.
3 Long, wavy, blond hair, brown eyes.
4 Short, curly, red hair, blue eyes.
5 Short, straight, brown hair, green eyes.
6 Short, spiky, brown hair, brown eyes.

> **WATCH OUT!**
> long/short   curly/straight
> blond/brown/dark/red hair
> big/small   blue/brown eyes

8 Which words in Exercise 4 describe your hair and eyes? Write them down. Tell a partner. Use the Watch out! box for help.

_____ _____ _____ hair
_____ _____ eyes

9 Work in pairs. Describe someone in your class. Guess who it is.
A: Long, straight, brown hair, brown eyes.
B: It's Alice!

YOUR WORLD
10 Do you know a person with …
a green eyes? *My mum.*   c spiky hair?
b grey hair?   d a small nose?

I can describe someone's face, eyes and hair.

4.2 Grammar
have got affirmative and negative

VIDEO ▶ **I HAVEN'T GOT BIG FEET!**

1 At the bookshop.

Alex: Ouch, my foot!
Jen: It isn't my fault! You've got long legs. And you've got big feet.
Alex: I haven't got big feet! I'm tall!

2

Jen: You've got long arms too.
Alex: Yeah, but I haven't got a big head, like you!

3

Jen: My head is fine! Mum?
Mum: Stop it, you two! Jen, your brother hasn't got big feet. Alex, your sister hasn't got a big head. Now, hurry up! We haven't got a lot of time.

4

Jen: Oh, they've got *Yummy Cupcakes*. Great! Oh, no! It's too high! Alex? Help me, please!

SOUNDS GOOD! It isn't my fault! • Stop it! • Help me, please!

1 ▶ 19 🔊 4.3 Watch the video. Then listen and read. Jen needs Alex's help. Why? Complete the sentence.

The book is too _____.

2 Choose the correct option.
1 *Alex* / Jen is tall.
2 Alex's arms are *long* / *short*.
3 Jen's head *is* / *isn't* big.
4 Jen's book is about *cupcakes* / *tall people*.

3 🔊 4.4 Listen and repeat. Find these expressions in the story.

4 Will Alex help Jen? Have a class vote.

5 ▶ 20 🔊 4.5 Now watch or listen and check.

Unit 4

6 Study the Grammar box. Then watch.

GRAMMAR — *have got* affirmative and negative

+ Short and long form	− Short and long form
I've (have) got long legs.	I haven't (have not) got long legs.
You've (have) got long legs.	You haven't (have not) got long legs.
He/She/It's (has) got long legs.	He/She/It hasn't (has not) got long legs.
We've (have) got long legs.	We haven't (have not) got long legs.
You've (have) got long legs.	You haven't (have not) got long legs.
They've (have) got long legs.	They haven't (have not) got long legs.

7 Complete the sentences with *'ve got* or *'s got*.
1. Jen: Alex, you *'ve got* big feet!
2. Jen: My brother _____ long arms.
3. Alex: Jen _____ a big head.
4. Jen: They _____ Yummy Cupcakes!
5. Mum: We _____ this book.

8 🔊 4.6 Listen and repeat.

VOCABULARY — Parts of the body

arm   body   fingers   foot   hand   head   leg

9 Match the parts of the body 1–7 with the words in the Vocabulary box.

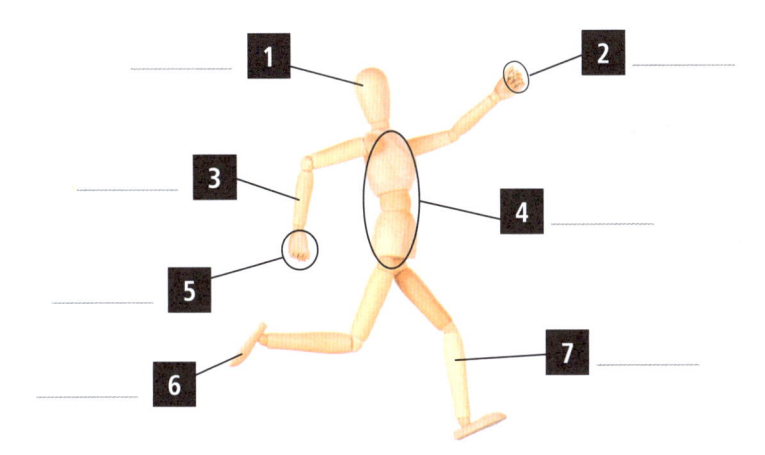

10 Write correct sentences in your notebook.
1. Jen's got blond hair. (brown)
   Jen hasn't got blond hair. She's got brown hair.
2. Alex has got small feet. (big)
3. Jen and Alex have got short legs. (long)
4. Jen and Alex's mum has got blue eyes. (brown)
5. Jen and Alex have got big heads. (small)

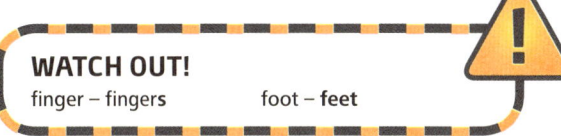

VIDEO ▶ 21 GET GRAMMAR!

I haven't got a hat.

WATCH OUT!
finger – finger**s**   foot – **feet**

11 Look at the picture. Complete the text with the words below.

big   feet   got   has   ~~have~~   tall   they

Ike   Mike

Ike and Mike [1] *have* got long, spiky hair.
[2] _____ have got big mouths, but they haven't got [3] _____ noses. Mike is [4] _____. He [5] _____ got green hair. He has [6] _____ very long arms and very big [7] _____.

12 Write about Ike. Use Exercise 11 for help.
Ike isn't tall. He's got …

YOUR WORLD

13 Draw a friend for Ike and Mike. Give her a name and describe her.
*Ike and Mike have got a friend. She's got … and …
She's got … , but she hasn't got …*

I can use the affirmative and negative forms of the verb *have got*.

4.3 Grammar
have got questions and short answers

The Terrific Two – My favourite superhero!

1

Ricky: Wonder Will is my favourite hero. He has got a super car. What have you got, Superdug? Have you got a super car?
Superdug: No, I haven't.
Ricky: Have you got a friend?
Superdug: Yes, I have. Her name's Kit.

2

Ricky: Wonder Will's got *two* friends. Their names are X1 and X2. They've got super ears. Has Kit got super ears?
Superdug: No, she hasn't.

3

Ricky: They've got super eyes too. Have you and Kit got super eyes?
Superdug: No, we haven't. Our eyes are like your eyes.

4

Ricky: X1 and X2 have got other super powers too!
Superdug: Yes, but have they got battery power?
Ricky: No, they haven't!

1 Look at the cartoon carefully. Someone looks like Superdug. Point at him/her.

2 🔊 4.7 Listen and read. Who is Wonder Will?

3 Read the sentences. Mark them T (true) or F (false).
1 Superdug is at home. T / F
2 Superdug hasn't got a super car. T / F
3 X1 and X2 have got super ears. T / F
4 Kit has got super eyes. T / F
5 X1 and X2 haven't got any battery power now. T / F

4 Study the Grammar box. Then watch.

GRAMMAR — *have got* questions and short answers

?	Short answers
Have I got a friend?	Yes, I have. / No, I haven't.
Have you got a friend?	Yes, you have. / No, you haven't.
Has he/she/it got a friend?	Yes, he/she/it has. / No, he/she/it hasn't.
Have we got a friend?	Yes, we have. / No, we haven't.
Have you got a friend?	Yes, you have. / No, you haven't.
Have they got a friend?	Yes, they have. / No, they haven't.

What have you got? I've got super powers!

VIDEO ▶ 22 GET GRAMMAR!

Have you got a brother or a sister?
Yes, I have!

5 Complete the questions. Use *have … got* or *has … got*.
1 *Has* Wonder Will *got* a red suit?
2 _____ Ricky _____ brown hair?
3 _____ X1 and X2 _____ big heads?
4 _____ Kit _____ brown eyes?
5 _____ X1 and X2 _____ long legs?
6 _____ Superdug _____ long ears?

6 Look at the cartoon on page 60. Answer the questions in Exercise 5 in your notebook.
1 *No, he hasn't.*

7 In pairs, ask and answer about the superheroes.

	super eyes	super ears	super arms
Wondercat	✓	✓	✗
Iron Girls	✓	✗	✓

A: Has Wondercat got super eyes?
B: Yes, she has.

WATCH OUT!
he → his   His superhero costume is green.
she → her   Her eyes are green.
it → its   Its eyes are blue.
we → our   Wonder Will is our friend!
you → your   Your hair is blond and spiky!
they → their Their noses are red.

8 Complete the sentences. Use *his*, *her*, *its*, *our* or *their*.
1 They've got green suits.
   These are *their* suits.
2 We've got a super car!
   This is _____ super car!
3 He's got a new robot.
   This is _____ new robot.
4 Has she got a super friend?
   Is this _____ super friend?
5 Has it got a battery?
   Is this _____ battery?

9 Work in pairs. Student A, ask Student B what he/she has got. Student B, answer the questions. Use the words below. Then change roles. Tell the class about your partner.

a brother or a sister?   a pet?   a TV in your room?
a friend?   a bike?   a robot?   a cousin?

10 🔊 4.8 🔊 4.9 Go to page 141. Listen and sing the Robots' Song.

YOUR WORLD

I can ask questions with the verb *have got* and use *his, her, its, our, your, their*.

4.4 Speaking
Apologising

VIDEO ▶ SORRY ABOUT THAT!

Dad: Where are my house keys?
Jen: I'm so sorry, Dad. I've got them.
Dad: It's OK. Now where's my phone? Oops! Sorry, Jen!
Jen: That's all right. Dad. You've got the phone. It's right there.
Dad: Sorry, my mistake!
Jen: No problem.
Dad: Oh, it's late! Bye, Jen!

Jen: Dad, wait! Your house keys!
Dad: Oh, dear! Sorry about that! Thanks, sweetie! Bye!
Jen: Bye, Dad!

Jen: Come on! Really? Erm … Dad?

1 ▶ 23 ◀)) 4.10 Watch the video. Then listen and read. Who has got Dad's phone? Choose the correct answer.
   a Jen   b Dad

2 ◀)) 4.11 Listen and repeat.

> **SPEAKING Apologising**
>
> **A:** I'm so sorry.   **B:** It's OK.
>   Sorry about that!   That's all right.
>   Sorry, my mistake.   No problem.

3 ◀)) 4.12 Complete the dialogues. Then listen and check. Act out the dialogues in pairs.
   1 **A:** Oops! Sorry about that, Pete!
      B: No *problem*.
   2 **A:** Where's my phone?
      B: _____! I've got it!
      A: That's _____.
   3 **A:** This isn't my jacket.
      B: Sorry, my _____. Here you are.
      A: _____ OK. Thanks.

4 Write dialogues for the pictures. Then act out the dialogues in pairs.

   1 **A:** Ouch!
      B: _____
      A: _____
   2 **A:** This isn't my bag.
      B: _____
      A: _____

YOUR WORLD

5 Make dialogues in pairs. Use expressions from the Speaking box. Then act out the dialogues in class.
   A: Where's my pen?
   B: I'm so sorry. I've got it.
   A: No problem.

I can say sorry and respond to an apology.

4.5 Reading and Vocabulary
Personality quiz

1 🔊 **4.13** Listen and repeat. Then complete the sentences with the words in the Vocabulary box.

> **VOCABULARY** Personality adjectives
>
> clever   friendly   funny   helpful   nice

1. I speak to everyone.
   I'm *friendly*.
2. My teacher helps me every day.
   She's _____.
3. You've got flowers for your mum.
   You're very _____.
4. My friend's jokes are great!
   He's _____.
5. My school grades are good.
   I'm _____.

2 Do the personality quiz! Choose a, b or c.

3 Count how many a, b and c answers you have got and read the key. Do you agree? Tell a friend or the class!

4 🔊 **4.14** Listen to two friends, Sue and Sam. Are they friendly, funny and clever? Tick (✓) for *yes* and put a cross (✗) for *no*.

	friendly	funny	clever
Sam	✓		
Sue			

5 Write about someone you like. Read out your text.

My neighbour Nico is very friendly and nice. He's funny too! His jokes are great!

What kind of person are you?
Are you funny? Are you friendly?

Quiz time
Do our personality quiz to find out!

1. How many good friends have you got?
   a 3–6   b 7–10   c 1 or 2
2. Are your jokes funny?
   a Sometimes.   b Yes!   c No. My jokes are bad!
3. What's your favourite place?
   a School.   b A party!   c My room.
4. Are you good at school?
   a I'm OK.   b Yes, I am!
   c I'm good at my favourite subjects.
5. Your best friend has got a problem. You
   a help your friend.   b just say 'I'm sorry'.
   c say 'Speak to your mum.'
6. Your neighbour has got a big bag. You say:
   a 'Let me help you!'   b 'That's big!'
   c 'I'm sorry, I've got homework.'

KEY:

A lot of your answers are **a**.

GOOD FRIEND!
You are a good friend. You are very nice! You are helpful and you are a good student.

A lot of your answers are **b**.

PARTY ANIMAL!
You are very funny and friendly, but you aren't always very helpful. Jokes, parties and dancing are your favourite things, but you are also a good student.

A lot of your answers are **c**.

HOME LOVER!
You are friendly . . . sometimes! You don't like groups and you aren't very helpful. You are usually a good student.

I can understand a text about personalities.

4.6 Listening and Writing
Your favourite cartoon character

1 Look at photos 1–4. Can you name the cartoons?

2 🔊 4.15 Find the characters in the photos. Write the correct number. There is one extra photo. Then listen and check.
- a ☐ Kevin
- b ☐ SpongeBob SquarePants
- c ☐ Skipper

3 🔊 4.16 Listen to the dialogue and tick (✓) the children's opinion.

	SpongeBob SquarePants	Kevin	Skipper
funny	✓	✓	
helpful			
friendly			
clever			

4 🔊 4.16 Listen again and complete the sentences with the words below.

> ~~clever~~   cool   friendly   Kevin   Skipper

1. SpongeBob SquarePants isn't very *clever*.
2. All Minions are _____.
3. _____ loves bananas and apples.
4. _____ has got good ideas.
5. Sometimes Skipper isn't nice or _____.

5 Who is your favourite cartoon character? Describe him/her to a friend.

6 Read Lian's text about her favourite cartoon character. Do you know him?

> **Paragraph 1** Kung Fu Panda's name is Po. He's got a big body and head. He's got big blue eyes and small black ears. His legs are short and his arms are long. He's got yellow and red shorts.
>
> **Paragraph 2** I think Po is nice. He's funny and he's friendly. He's got lots of friends. He's clever and he's very good at kung fu!

7 Study the Writing box. Then read Lian's text in Exercise 6 again. Write the paragraph numbers. Add examples from Lian's text to each paragraph.
- ☐ Face and body *big body, big head, …*
- ☐ Personality *nice, …*

WRITING · Paragraphs
A paragraph is a part of a text. It is about one main idea. Remember to divide your text into paragraphs!

WRITING TIME

8 Write about your favourite character from a book or cartoon.

1 Find ideas
Find a photo of your character. Make a list of words describing his/her face, body and personality.

2 Draft
Write a paragraph describing his/her face and body.
(Your character's name) has got long, straight, blond hair …
Write a paragraph about his/her personality.
He/She isn't very clever, but …

3 Check and write
Check the paragraphs and write the final version of your text.

Unit 4 · 64 · I can understand and write short texts about cartoon characters.

4.7 CLIL: Science
Genes

WATCH OUT!
Which picture shows genes?

EYE COLOUR
HAIR COLOUR

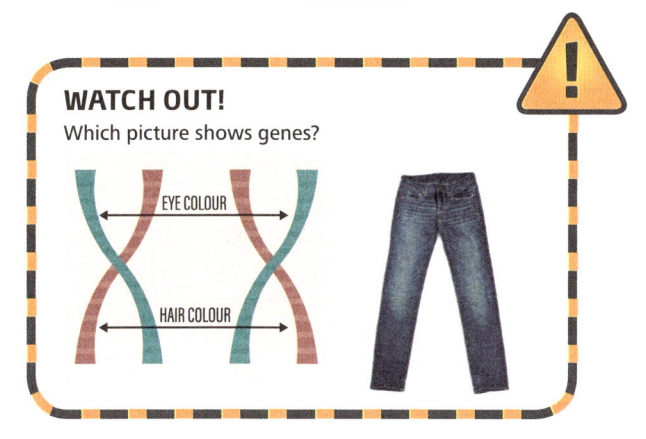

1 🔊 4.17 Listen and repeat.

VOCABULARY — Adjectives

different   same   strong   weak

2 Read the text and find the words in the Vocabulary box. In pairs, discuss what they mean. Check with your teacher.

PAUL
Hair: bl bl (blond)
Eyes: B b (brown)

SOPHIE
Hair: D bl (dark)
Eyes: b b (blue)

DAD
Hair: D bl (dark)
Eyes: B b (brown)

MUM
Hair: bl bl (blond)
Eyes: b b (blue)

D = dark   bl = blond
D = strong   bl = weak
B = brown   b = blue
B = strong   b = weak

IT'S IN THE GENES!

Sophie and Paul are brother and sister. They haven't got the same hair and eye colour. Sophie has got dark hair and blue eyes. Paul has got blond hair and brown eyes. That's because they've got a different combination of genes from their parents.
We have got two genes for our hair colour and two genes for our eye colour. One gene is from our mother and one gene is from our father.
We get different colours from different gene combinations. For example, here, brown eye genes (B) are strong (dominant) and blue eye genes (b) are weak (recessive). People with two B genes have got brown eyes. People with one B gene and one b gene have also got brown eyes because B is strong. People with two b genes have got blue eyes.

3 Read the text again and write the hair or eye colour for the gene combinations.
1 D D _dark_
2 D bl _____
3 bl bl _____
4 B B _____
5 B b _____
6 b b _____

4 In pairs, read the sentences. Mark them T (true) or F (false).
1 We get our genes from our brothers and sisters. T / F
2 The colour of our eyes is from a combination of two genes. T / F
3 The genes for hair colour are not the same as the genes for eye colour. T / F
4 Brothers and sisters always have the same combination of genes. T / F

5 Colour Leon's hair and Fergie's eyes.

B = brown, strong   g = green, weak   r = red, weak

r r —
B g — Mum

B r
g g Dad

B r
B g — Leon

r r
g g Fergie

YOUR WORLD

6 Draw you and your family. What colour eyes and hair have you got? Guess the gene combinations.

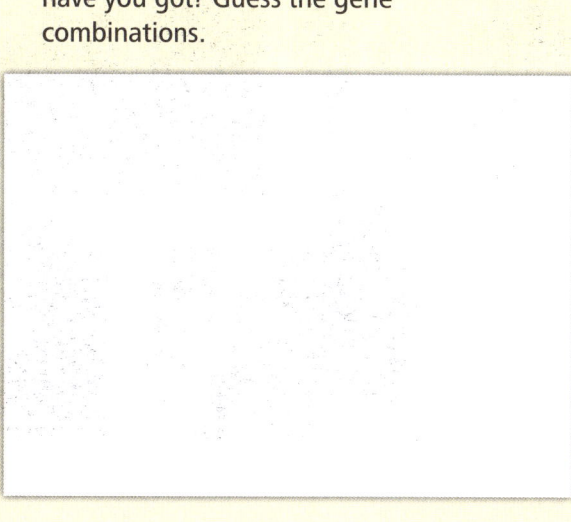

I can understand gene combinations.

Vocabulary Activator

WORDLIST 4.18

Face, eyes, hair
blond (adj)
blue (adj)
brown (adj)
curly (adj)
dark (adj)
ears (n)
eyes (n)
face (n)
green (adj)
grey (adj)
mouth (n)
nose (n)
red (adj)
spiky (adj)
straight (adj)
wavy (adj)

Parts of the body
arm (n)
body (n)
fingers (n)
foot (plural: feet) (n)
hand (n)
head (n)
leg (n)

Personality adjectives
clever (adj)
friendly (adj)
funny (adj)
helpful (adj)
nice (adj)

Adjectives
different (adj)
same (adj)
strong (adj)
weak (adj)

Extra words
a lot of (quantifier)
always (adv)
answer (n)
battery power
combination (n)
dancing (n)
do a quiz
fine (adj)
gene (n)
good at
good student
group (n)
Help me, please!
high (adj)
home lover
homework (n)
house key
How many?
Hurry up!
It isn't my fault!
joke (n)
long (adj)
like (prep)
Oh, dear!
Ouch!
party animal (n)
person (n)
personality (n)
place (n)
room (n)
say (v)
short (adj)
sometimes (adv)
speak (v)
Stop it!
subject (n)
super power (n)
sweetie (n)
tall (adj)
time (n)
usually (adv)
What kind of …?

1 Tick (✓) the correct phrases and put a cross (✗) for the incorrect phrases.
1 wavy ears ✓
2 straight head
3 long nose
4 curly mouth
5 funny boy
6 spiky arm
7 nice girl
8 blond eyes

2 Whose face and body parts are they? The clues are on page 58.

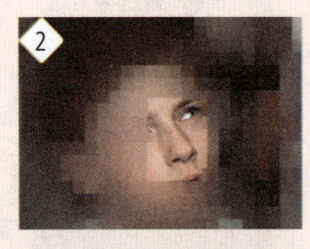

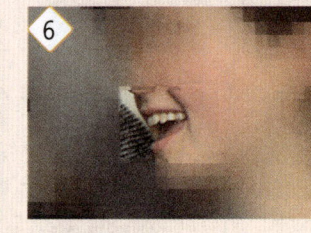

1 *They're Jen's legs.*

3 Describe the people. Use personality adjectives from the wordlist.
1 Maria: Let me help you!
   Maria is *helpful*.
2 Theo: This cake is for you.
   Theo is _____ .
3 You: Ha! Ha! Great joke, Charlie!
   Charlie is _____ .
4 Alex: Hi! Great to see you! How are you?
   Alex is _____ .
5 Isabella: I'm good at Chinese, Spanish and French.
   Isabella is _____ .

4 4.19 **PRONUNCIATION** /h/
Listen and repeat.
Her name's Helpful Helen.
Her horse's name is Claire.
Her home is in Hastings.
She's got dark hair!

Revision

Vocabulary

1 Look at Maddy and write the parts of the body 1–8 in your notebook. Then complete words a–d.

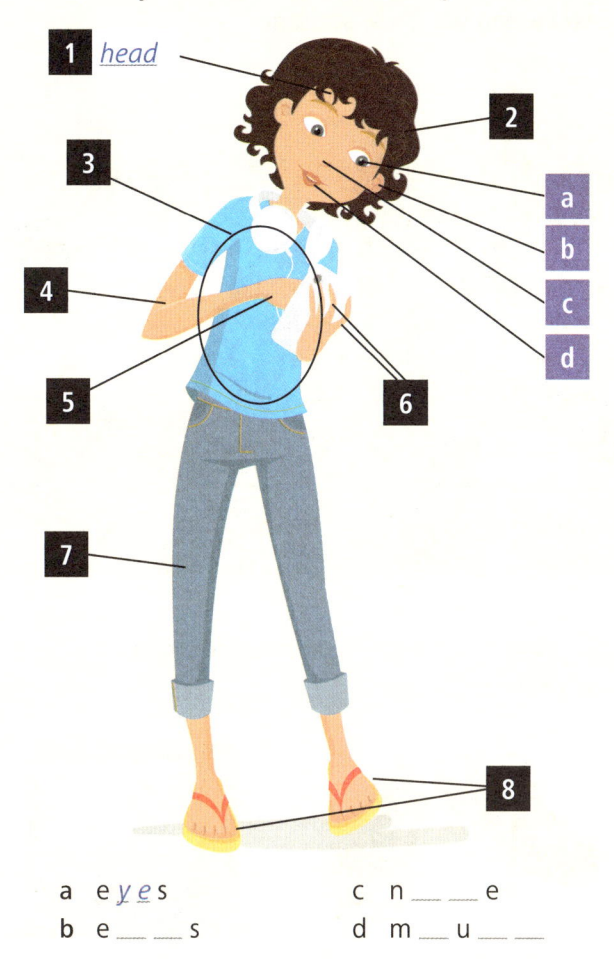

1 head

a e y e s
b e ___ s
c n ___ e
d m ___ u ___ ___

2 Read sentences 1–3 about Maddy's hair. Tick (✓) the sentence that is true.
1 ☐ She's got long, dark, straight hair.
2 ☐ She's got short, blond, wavy hair.
3 ☐ She's got short, brown, curly hair.

3 Match the letters to make five adjectives.

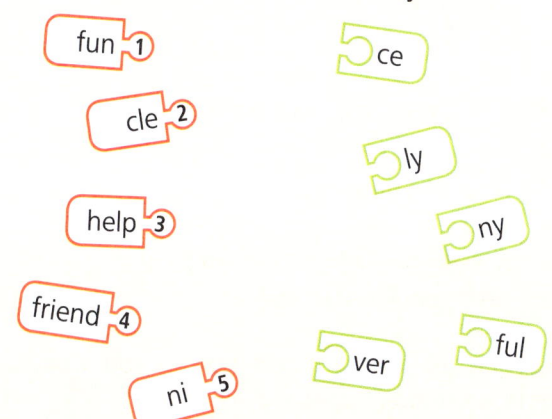

fun 1, cle 2, help 3, friend 4, ni 5
ce, ly, ny, ver, ful

Grammar

4 Complete the sentences with *have/has got* (✓) or *haven't/hasn't got* (✗).
1 Kit _____ big, green eyes. ✓
2 Lucas _____ blond hair. His hair is dark. ✗
3 My brother and I _____ long legs. ✓
4 I _____ curly hair. My hair is straight. ✗
5 Lian _____ brown eyes. ✓

5 Make questions with *have/has got* in your notebook.
1 you / brown eyes?
   Have you got brown eyes?
2 your dad / curly hair?
3 you and your friends / dark hair?
4 your mum / long arms?
5 your parents / blue eyes?
6 your grandparents / a pet?

6 Answer the questions in Exercise 4.
1 Yes, I have./No, I haven't.

7 Complete the sentences with *his, her, its, our, your* or *their*.
1 A: What are *your* names, please?
   B: _____ names are Jo and Frankie.
2 A: Is that Lisa and _____ friend?
   B: That's right. _____ name's Andrew.
3 Oh, look at that cat! One of _____ eyes is green and the other is blue!
4 This is a photo of my aunt and uncle, and this is _____ new house.

Speaking

8 Complete the dialogues with the words below.

| it's OK   mistake   problem   so   sorry   that's |

1 A: This isn't my phone.
   B: Sorry, my ¹*mistake*. Here you are.
   A: ² _____ all right.
2 A: Where's my cap?
   B: Oops! I've got it. ³ _____ about that.
   A: No ⁴ _____ .
3 A: I haven't got your book today. I'm ⁵ _____ sorry.
   B: ⁶ _____ .

67 Unit 4

SET FOR LIFE

Keeping things tidy

1 Look at pictures A and B. Describe them and say how you feel when you look at them. Use the expressions below.

> It's messy / organised and tidy.   I feel relaxed / stressed.

A

B

2 In pairs, cross (✗) the items you do not have on an organised desk.

1. ☐ a toothbrush
2. ☐ a ruler
3. ☐ a box of cereal
4. ☐ swimming goggles
5. ☐ a pen holder with pens
6. ☐ a sticky tape dispenser

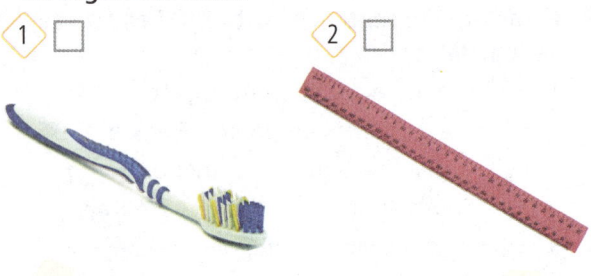

3 In pairs, discuss the right place for items A–D in a tidy room.

A a pair of trainers
B a laptop
C a set of keys
D a schoolbook

4 🔊 4.20 Listen and write *Sam*, *Trina*, *Ted* or *Lisa*.
1. Who is organised? _____
2. Who isn't organised? _____
3. Who feels relaxed in Harry's room? _____
4. Who feels stressed because he/she hasn't got something? _____

5 Choose the option that is true for you. Compare your answers in pairs.
1. My desk is *organised / messy*. *It's easy / It isn't easy* to study or do my homework.
2. My bedroom is *messy / tidy*. I feel *relaxed / stressed* when I'm in it.

Units 3–4   68   I can be tidy.

6 Read the Useful Tips and complete the sentences.

```
• • •   ← →  C
```

BIG PROJECT?

No problem!

Before
1 _____ a list of the things you need.
2 Put _____ all the things you need.
3 _____ for the things you haven't got.

After
4 Put the things _____ in the right place.

7 🔊 4.20 Listen again. Give Sam and Lisa two useful tips each. Use ideas from Exercise 6.
1 Sam, _____ in your bag the night before football practice.
_____. Then it's easy to find them.
2 Lisa, _____ for your project.
_____ the laptop.

SET FOR LIFE

8 In groups, make a class poster with useful tips about how to be organised. Follow these steps.

1 In your group, suggest some tips. Look up the words you need.

2 Choose six tips for your poster. Find photos or draw pictures if you want.

3 Make your poster. Be organised! Use your own tips to help you. 🙂

4 Present your poster to the class. Discuss the tips in the other posters.

Be tidy!

USEFUL TIPS

It's important to be tidy and organised at school and at home.

Make a list of the things you need.

Put together all the things you need.

Ask for things you haven't got

Be tidy. Put things back in their place.

Progress Check Units 1–4

Vocabulary and Grammar

1 Choose the correct answer.
1. George's dad's sister's daughter is his
   a sister.   b aunt.   c cousin.
2. Mum's car is in the
   a fridge.   b garage.   c carpet.
3. Kate is very tall. Her _____ and legs are long.
   a eyes   b hair   c arms
4. Lisa's test is 10/10. She's very
   a nice.   b clever.   c helpful.
5. My _____ under my nose.
   a mouth is   b ears are   c eyes are
6. This _____ is big. It's for four people.
   a sofa   b chair   c wall

2 Complete the dialogue with one word in each gap.

Bart: Look at this photo.
Ellie: Who are ¹ *those* people?
Bart: Harry, my best friend, and ² _____ family. They're a big family.
Ellie: How many people ³ _____ there in Harry's family?
Bart: Seven. He's ⁴ _____ four brothers.
Ellie: ⁵ _____ he got a sister?
Bart: No, he ⁶ _____.
Ellie: Is that his living room in the photo?
Bart: Yes, it ⁷ _____. Harry's living room is very cool!
Ellie: ⁸ _____ are a lot of film posters on the walls.
Bart: They're Harry's dad's. He's a film star!

3 Read the sentences and complete the words.
1. Nadia's hair isn't curly or wavy. It's *straight*.
2. He's from the UK. He's B_____.
3. They're for your feet. They're tr_____.
4. A ba_____ is a room in your house.
5. We've got two hands and ten f_____.
6. A f_____ is usually in the kitchen.
7. C_____ are usually on sofas, armchairs and beds.
8. I'm not at home. I'm not at school. I'm on h_____!

Speaking

4 Read the dialogues. Choose the correct answer.

Jane: Hi, come in!
Peter: ¹ _____
Jane: Would you like some orange juice?
Peter: ² _____ Oops! Oh, no! My juice is on the floor!
Jane: ³ _____

Alisha: Olga, this is my brother, Tad.
Olga: ⁴ _____
Tad: Nice to meet you too, Olga. Where are you from?
Olga: ⁵ _____

1. a No problem.   b Are you OK?
   c) Thanks.
2. a Yes, I have.   b No, I'm not.
   c Yes, please.
3. a I'm fine, thank you.   b That's all right.
   c It's nice.
4. a Very well, thanks.   b Nice to meet you, Tad.
   c What's your name?
5. a Poland.   b In the living room.
   c No, I'm Polish.

5 Work in pairs.
1. Describe your favourite room in your house.
2. Describe your favourite person in your family. Talk about:
   - their face, eyes and hair
   - their body
   - their personality

Listening

6 🔊 **4.21** Listen and draw lines. There is one extra picture.

Reading

7 In pairs, say what you can see in photos A–C in Exercise 8.

8 Read the blog. Match texts 1–3 with photos A–C.

✉️

What's your favourite place? Write about it!

Cora, 13
1 My favourite place is my grandmother's cottage. I love the living room. It's got big windows, Granny's favourite yellow armchair, a lot of pictures on the walls and a lot of books. Granny isn't old. She's got long, brown hair and blue eyes, like me. She's very nice and she's funny too!

Yasmin, 11
2 My favourite place is our classroom! It's very big and it's got long, brown desks. We've all got boxes for our books and schoolbags.

Julia, 12
3 My favourite place is our holiday home in the country. I go there with my mum, dad and sister. It's got two small bedrooms, a living room, a kitchen and a bathroom. My sister and I love the garden.

9 Read the sentences. Mark them Y (yes) or N (no).
1 Cora's granny's house is a cottage. Y / N
2 Cora's old books are in the living room. Y / N
3 Yasmin's classroom is small. Y / N
4 In Yasmin's classroom, there are boxes for the students' things. Y / N
5 Julia's holiday home has got five rooms. Y / N
6 Julia hasn't got a sister. Y / N

Writing

10 Write 40–50 words about your favourite place. Use these questions to help you.
1 What is your favourite place?
2 Where is this place? What rooms has it got?
3 What nice things are there in it?
4 Who is there? Say a few words about them.

My favourite place is … It's in …
There are … in my favourite place.
There is a nice … / There are nice …

Things I can do

5

VOCABULARY
Action verbs | make, play, ride |
Language | Musical instruments

GRAMMAR
can affirmative and negative | can questions and short answers

5.1 Vocabulary
Action verbs

1 Find the actions below in the photos.

| dance draw fix jump ride run swim |

Unit 5 72

2 🔊 **5.1** Listen and repeat. Which action verbs are not in the photos on page 72?

VOCABULARY	Action verbs
act cook dance draw fix fly jump read	
ride run sing swim write	

3 Match six words from the Vocabulary box with pictures 1–6.

1 _____
2 _____
3 _____
4 _____
5 _____
6 _____

4 🔊 **5.2** Listen to the sounds and choose the correct option.
 1 write / (read)
 2 swim / cook
 3 draw / ride
 4 write / fly
 5 run / fix
 6 sing / act

5 Which actions 1–8 are in the picture? Tick (✓) for *yes* or put a cross (✗) for *no*.

 1 ✓ swim   5 ☐ draw
 2 ☐ dance   6 ☐ fix
 3 ☐ read   7 ☐ ride
 4 ☐ jump   8 ☐ fly

6 In pairs, look at the picture in Exercise 5. Mime actions for your partner to guess!

7 In pairs, write the actions.
 1 Things we do at school: *read, write, draw*
 2 Things actors do: _____
 3 Things we do at home: _____
 4 Things we do for sport: _____
 5 Things birds do: _____

YOUR WORLD

8 Make two lists that are true for you. Use the Vocabulary box to help you.

 I think it's easy to: *cook,* _____
 I think it's difficult to: _____

I can understand and use action verbs.   **73**   Unit 5

5.2 Grammar
can affirmative and negative

VIDEO ▶ I CAN FIX IT!

1
Lian: Guys, this video is for my granny in Shanghai. Granny Lin, this is my friend, Lucas.
Lucas: Hello!
Lian: Lucas can play the guitar and he can sing!
Lucas: I can't sing very well, but …

2
Lian: Oh, no, not again!
Alex: What's wrong?
Lian: It's the camera. I can't see a thing!
Alex: Let me see … Hmm, I can fix it.
Lian: Thanks! Alex is a genius! He can fix things. He can do very clever things with computers too.

3
Jen: Yes, very clever – he can play computer games all day! Cupcake?
Lian: Jen is a fantastic cook! These cupcakes are yummy!

4
Alex: But what about Lian?
Lucas: Yes, what can she do?

1 ▶ 24 ◀)) 5.3 Watch the video. Then listen and read. Complete the sentence.

There's something wrong with Lian's _____ .

SOUNDS GOOD! Not again! • What's wrong? • Let me see …

2 Complete the sentences.
1 The video is for *Lian's granny*.
2 Lian's granny is in _____ .
3 _____ is a genius.
4 _____ is a good cook.

3 ◀)) 5.4 Listen and repeat. Find these expressions in the story.

4 What can Lian do? Clue 1: Look at photo 3. Clue 2: Look at the picture of the elephant in photo 4.

Lian can s __ __ __ __ __ __ __ d and d __ __ w!

5 ▶ 25 ◀)) 5.5 Now watch or listen and check.

Unit 5

6 Study the Grammar box. Then watch.

GRAMMAR — can affirmative and negative

+	−
I can jump.	I can't jump.
You can jump.	You can't jump.
He/She/It can jump.	He/She/It can't jump.
We can jump.	We can't jump.
You can jump.	You can't jump.
They can jump.	They can't jump.

VIDEO ▶ 26 GET GRAMMAR!

"I can't dance, but I can jump!"

7 Who can do these things? Complete the sentences with the names below. Then look at the photos on page 74 and check.

Alex (x1)   Jen (x2)   Lian (x2)   Lucas (x2)

1 *Lian can* skateboard.
2 _____ _____ sing.
3 _____ _____ play computer games.
4 _____ _____ make cupcakes.
5 _____ _____ draw.
6 _____ _____ cook.
7 _____ _____ play the guitar.

8 Follow the lines and complete the sentences with *can* or *can't*. Then read the sentences.

1 Lian *can't fix things*.
2 Jen _____ .   draw
3 Alex _____ .   cook
4 Lucas _____ .   play the guitar
5 Lian _____ .   fix things
6 Alex _____ .   skateboard
                                   sing

9 🔊 5.6 Listen and choose the correct option.
1 He can / (can't) swim.
2 She can / can't draw.
3 They can / can't act.
4 He can / can't sing.
5 She can / can't run.
6 His brother can / can't read.

10 🔊 5.7 Listen and repeat.

VOCABULARY — make, play, ride

make   a poster/cupcakes
play   computer games/football/the piano
ride   a bike/a horse

WATCH OUT!
play volleyball   play **the** piano

11 Complete Lucas's email with *can* and *make*, *play* or *ride*.

Here's what my family can do. My dad ¹*can play* football very well. My mum ² _____ _____ a horse and she ³ _____ _____ the piano. My aunt Melina ⁴ _____ _____ cupcakes. They're yummy! As for me, I ⁵ _____ _____ the guitar and I ⁶ _____ _____ a bike.

YOUR WORLD

12 Work in pairs. Student A, write three true and three false sentences. Student B, guess which sentences are true. Then change roles and have the conversation again.
A: My granny can skateboard.
B: No, she can't!

I can use the verb *can* in affirmative and negative sentences.

5.3 Grammar

can questions and short answers

The Terrific Two – Thank you, Superdug!

1
Dug: Ah, what a lovely day!

2
TOM! SUSAN!
Dug: Who's Tom and Susan?
Kit: Can you see the boat over there?
Dug: Yes, I can.
Kit: I think they are in it. Look!

3
Woman: Oh, no! My son and daughter can't swim! Can you help?
Kit: What can we do? Dug?!
Dug: What? Oh, yes. We can help! One minute, please.

4
Kit: That's Superdug!
Woman: He can run fast!
Kit: Yes, he can. He's a superhero!
Woman: Can he swim?
Kit: Oh! No, he can't …

5
Kit: He can't swim, but he can fly!

6
Woman: Thank you, Superdug!
Superdug: No problem!

1 Look at the cartoon and answer the questions.
  1 What is the title of Dug's book?
  2 Who can swim in the cartoon?

2 🔊 5.8 Listen and read. Complete the sentence.
  The woman is Tom and Susan's _____.

3 Read the cartoon again and complete the sentences with one word in each gap.
  1 Dug can <u>see</u> the boat.
  2 Susan and Tom are in the _____.
  3 Susan and Tom can't _____.
  4 Kit and Superdug _____ help.
  5 Superdug can't swim, but he can _____.

Unit 5   76

4 Study the Grammar box. Then watch.

GRAMMAR: can questions and short answers

?	Short answers
Can I swim?	Yes, I can. / No, I can't.
Can you swim?	Yes, you can. / No, you can't.
Can he/she/it swim?	Yes, he/she/it can. / No, he/she/it can't.
Can we swim?	Yes, we can. / No, we can't.
Can you swim?	Yes, you can. / No, you can't.
Can they swim?	Yes, they can. / No, they can't.

What can we do? We can help.

VIDEO ▶ **27 GET GRAMMAR!**

Can he run fast?
No, he can't.

5 Complete the questions and short answers.
1. A: *Can* Superdug *fly*? (fly)
   B: Yes, *he can*.
2. A: _____ Dug _____? (swim)
   B: No, _____ _____.
3. A: _____ you _____ the boat? (see)
   B: Yes, _____ _____.
4. A: _____ the little dog _____? (swim)
   B: Yes, _____ _____.

6 Look at the cartoon on page 76. In pairs, ask and answer the questions.
1. Picture 2: Dug / see the children?
   A: Can Dug see the children?
   B: Yes, he can.
2. Picture 3: Tom and Susan / swim?
3. Picture 3: What / Kit and Dug / do?
4. Picture 4: Superdug / run fast?
5. Picture 4: Superdug / swim?

7 In pairs, ask and answer about Kit and Dug.

	Kit	Dug
swim?	✓	✗
draw?	✗	✓
cook?	✓	✗

A: Can Kit swim?
B: Yes, she can.

8 Copy the table. Add your idea for number 5. Ask five classmates. How many can do these things? How many can't do these things?

Can you swim? Yes, I can. No, I can't.

Can you …	1	2	3	4	5
1 swim?	✓	✗	✓	✗	✗
2 fix a computer?					
3 ride a horse?					
4 draw?					
5 … ?					

9 Write about your classmates' answers in Exercise 8.
Two people can swim, and three people can't swim.

YOUR WORLD

10 🔊 5.9 🔊 5.10 Go to page 141. Listen and chant the Activities Rap.

I can ask and answer questions with the verb *can*. 77 Unit 5

5.4 Speaking
Suggestions

VIDEO ▶ LET'S DO SOMETHING FUN!

Lucas: Hey, guys, let's do something fun.
Jen: I agree. Any ideas?
Alex: We can go to the park.
Jen: Again? It's not a good idea.
Lian: Let's go ice-skating.
Jen: Great idea!
Lucas: I'm not sure … I can't skate very well.
Lian: No problem. I can teach you.
Lucas: OK, cool! Let's do that!

Alex: Hey, Lucas! You can wear these!
Lucas: Ha, ha! You're so funny!

1 ▶ 28 🔊 5.11 Watch the video. Then listen and read. What do they agree to do? Tick (✓) the correct photo.

1 ☐   2 ☐   3 ☐

2 🔊 5.12 Listen and repeat.

SPEAKING Suggestions

A: Let's *do something fun*!/Let's *go ice-skating*!/
We can *go to the park*!

B: 🙂 I agree!/Let's do that!/Great idea!
😐 I'm not sure.
☹ It's not a good idea.

3 Complete the sentences with one word in each gap.
1 We *can* go to the cinema!
2 _____ go to the swimming pool!
3 Let's _____ something fun!
4 _____ can play football!
5 We _____ ride our bikes!

4 Choose the best answer.
1 A: Let's do something fun.
  B: a Let me see …
     b I agree. Any ideas?
     c What's wrong?
2 A: Let's go to the swimming pool!
  B: a We can go to the park.
     b Let's do something fun.
     c I'm not sure … I can't swim very well.
3 A: No problem. I can teach you.
  B: a Yes, we can.
     b OK. Let's do that!
     c I can't do that.

5 Complete the dialogues with expressions from the Speaking box.
1 A: We can make cupcakes!   B: 🙂 *Great idea!*
2 A: Let's do something fun! B: 🙂 _____
3 A: We can go to the park.   B: ☹ _____
4 A: Let's play volleyball.   B: 😐 _____

6 In pairs, make dialogues like those in Exercise 5. Use the ideas below and add your own.

| go to the cinema   go to the swimming pool |
| make a video   play computer games |
| play volleyball   ride our bikes |

A: *Let's ride our bikes!*
B: *I agree!*

I can make suggestions about what to do.

5.5 Reading and Vocabulary
Sign language

1 🔊 **5.13** Listen and repeat. Match the words in the Vocabulary box with pictures 1–6.

VOCABULARY — Language

hear   language   learn   sign language   speak   special

1 _____   2 _____   3 _____
4 _____   5 _____   6 _____

2 Read the text quickly. What is it about? Choose the correct answer.
  a   Learn to speak Spanish
  b   Sign language
  c   Make things with your hands

3 🔊 **5.14** Read and listen to the text. Match headings a–d with paragraphs 1–4.
  a   Learn sign language!
  b   A special language
  c   Where is sign language important?
  d   What is sign language?

1 ☐ At school you can learn different languages, like English, French or Spanish. But there are special schools where teachers and students use sign language.

2 ☐ In sign language you make letters and words with your hands. It's for people who can't hear.

3 ☐ Sign language is important in schools and at home. All the family can learn sign language. They can speak to children who can't hear.

4 ☐ Are there children at your school who can't hear? Here's an idea: you can learn sign language and speak to them.

4 Read the sentences. Mark them T (true) or F (false).

1 People who can't hear have got a special language.   T / F
2 There are special schools for students who use sign language.   T / F
3 In sign language you draw pictures.   T / F
4 People who can hear can use sign language too.   T / F
5 People use sign language only in school.   T / F

5 Pictures 1–7 show a word in the British Sign Language alphabet. Go to page 142 and check the word. Practise saying the word with your hands.

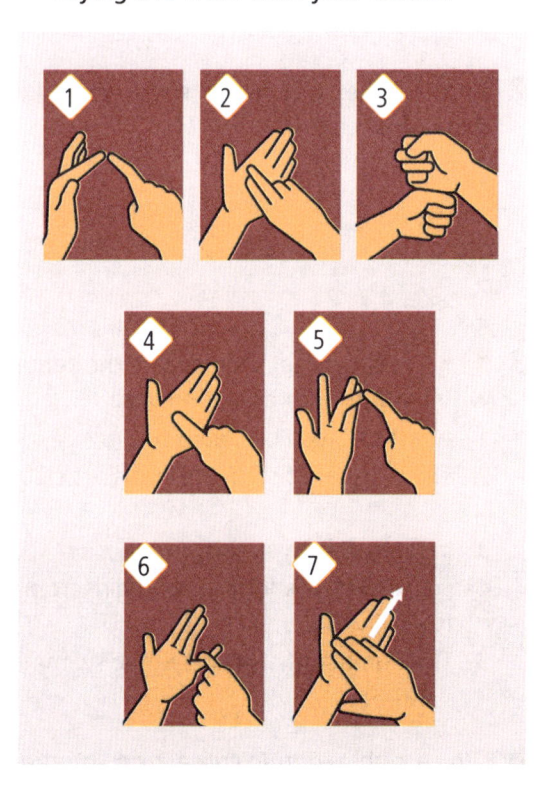

6 Spell your name in British Sign Language.

I can understand a text about sign language.   **79** Unit 5

5.6 Listening and Writing
After-school clubs

1 Match photos 1–4 with after-school clubs a–d. In pairs, say what you can do in these clubs.

a ☐ swimming club c ☐ drama club
b ☐ art club d ☐ football club

2 🔊 5.15 Listen and match speakers 1–4 with clubs a–d in Exercise 1.

Speaker 1 ☐
Speaker 2 ☐
Speaker 3 ☐
Speaker 4 ☐

3 🔊 5.15 Listen again. Complete the sentences with a number or an action verb.
1 At art club you can learn to *draw*.
2 The number of students in the art club is _____.
3 In drama club you learn to _____.
4 Football club is for boys and girls from twelve to _____.
5 The number of students in the swimming club is _____.

4 Which club a–d in Exercise 2 do you prefer?

5 Read the ad for an after-school club. Complete the sentence.

The club is for students who like _____.

> **COME TO COMPUTER CLUB!**
> You can write emails, but you can't write computer programs? We can teach you!
> You can make robots and you can play computer games too. How cool is that!
>
> **Where:** St Alban's Secondary School
> **When:** Monday, 4 o'clock
>
> See you there!
> www.U-and_Bot.get

6 Study the Writing box. Find *and* and *but* in the ad in Exercise 5.

> **WRITING** — Linkers: *and*, *but*
>
> You can make robots **and** you can play computer games.
> You can write emails, **but** you can't write computer programs.

7 Complete the sentences with *and* or *but*.
1 I can run *and* I can jump.
2 She can sing, _____ she can't act.
3 They can play computer games _____ make a robot, _____ they can't write computer programs.

WRITING TIME

8 Write an ad for an after-school club.

1 Find ideas
Make notes about what you can do at the club, and where and when the club is.

2 Draft
Give your ad a title: *Come to … Club!*
Write a paragraph about what you can do at the club.
You can … and …
You can … , but you can't …
Write where and when the club is.
Where: … When: … o'clock
Write the end. *See you there!*

3 Check and write
Check the linkers *(and, but)* and write the final version of your text.

I can understand and write short texts about after-school clubs.

5.7 CLIL: MUSIC
Musical instruments

1 🔊 5.16 Listen and repeat. Match the words in the Vocabulary box with photos 1–6.

VOCABULARY — Musical instruments

acoustic guitar   drums   electric guitar
keyboard   violin

1 _____   2 _____   3 _____

4 _____   5 _____

2 Read the quiz. Mark the sentences T (true) or F (false). Check your answers on page 142. What is your score?

3 Correct the false sentences in the quiz. Use the words below.

body   can't   China   feet   ~~Spain~~   wooden

1 The acoustic guitar is from *Spain*.
2 When you play the acoustic guitar, its _____ is on your legs.
3 Two-year-old children _____ learn to play the violin.
4 You can play the drums with your hands and _____ .
5 The violin is a _____ instrument.
6 The drums are from _____ .

4 Read the text. Answer Jane's question.

Hi, I'm Jane. I love music! Can you guess the instrument I can play? It's wooden and it's big. I play this instrument with my fingers. It's brown and black.

5 Imagine you can play one of the instruments from the quiz and complete the sentences. Use Exercise 4 to help.

I can play the _____ . It's _____ and _____ . I play this instrument with my _____ .

Quiz time!

1	The acoustic guitar is from France.	T / F
2	The guitar has got a head, a neck and a body.	T / F
3	When you play the acoustic guitar, its head is on your legs.	T / F
4	Two-year-old children can learn to play the violin.	T / F
5	You can only play the drums with your hands.	T / F
6	The violin is a glass instrument.	T / F
7	The keyboard is an electric instrument.	T / F
8	The body of the electric guitar is usually wooden.	T / F
9	The violin and the acoustic guitar are in the same family of instruments.	T / F
10	The drums are from the USA.	T / F

My score is __ / 10

I can name and describe musical instruments.

Vocabulary Activator

WORDLIST 🔊 5.17

Action verbs
act (v)
cook (v)
dance (v)
draw (v)
fix (v)
fly (v)
jump (v)
read (v)
ride (v)
run (v)
sing (v)
swim (v)
write (v)

make, play, ride
make cupcakes
make a poster

play computer games
play football
play the piano
ride a bike
ride a horse

Language
hear (v)
language (n)
learn (v)
sign language (n)
speak (v)
special (adj)

Musical instruments
acoustic guitar (n)
drums (n)
electric guitar (n)

keyboard (n)
violin (n)

Extra words
after-school (adj)
all day
boat (n)
camera (n)
club (n)
come (v)
fast (adv)
football (n)
game (n)
guys (n)
I can't see a thing.
important (adj)
Let me see …
letter (n)

lovely day
Not again!
One minute, please.
star (n)
teach (v)
teacher (n)
video (n)
volleyball (n)
wear (v)
well (adv)
What's wrong?
who (pronoun)
word (n)

1 Guess the action verbs.

1 _swim_
2 _____ 
3 _____ 
4 _____ 
5 _____ 
6 _____ 
7 _____ 
8 _____ 

2 Complete the words from the wordlist.

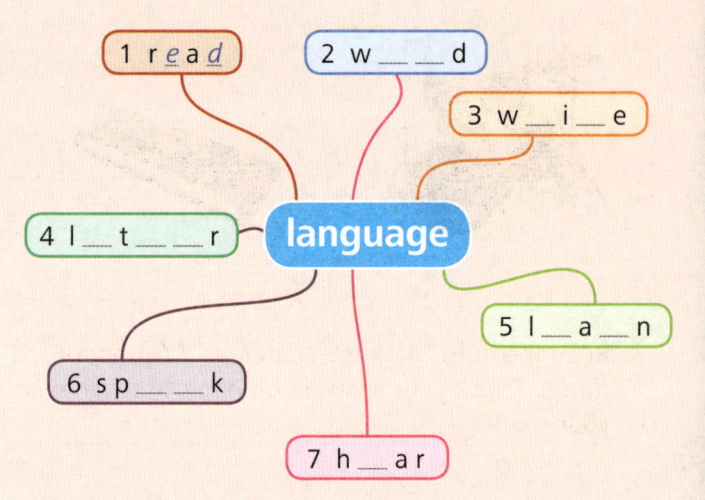

1 r e a d
2 w ___ ___ d
3 w ___ i ___ e
4 l ___ t ___ ___ r
5 l ___ a ___ n
6 s p ___ ___ k
7 h ___ ar

language

3 Find the words and phrases in the wordlist that have something to do with music, sports and food.
   1 music: _dance,_ _____
   2 sports: _____
   3 food: _____

4 🔊 5.18 **PRONUNCIATION** /æ/, /ɑː/
Listen and repeat.
Mark's Aunt Ann can play the guitar.
But she can't sing or act so she isn't a star!

Revision

Vocabulary

1 Look at the picture and complete the action verbs 1–8. Then write five more action verbs in your notebook.

1 f *l* y
2 a _ t
3 f _ x
4 s _ _ g
5 j _ _ p
6 r _ n
7 s _ _ m
8 r _ _ d

2 Complete the phrases with *make*, *play* or *ride*.
1 *make* cupcakes
2 _____ a bike
3 _____ the guitar
4 _____ football
5 _____ a horse
6 _____ a poster

3 Complete the sentences with the words below.

| cupcakes guitar hear learn speak ~~special~~ |

1 Sign language is a *special* language for people who can't _____ .
2 We can _____ Spanish or French at our school.
3 I can read French, but I can't _____ it very well.
4 I can play the _____ and I can make yummy _____ too.

Grammar

4 In your notebook, write sentences with *can* (✓) or *can't* (✗) and *and* or *but*.
1 Superdug / fly ✓ / swim ✗
   Superdug can fly, but he can't swim.
2 Leo / play the piano ✗ / play football ✓
3 I / make a cake ✗ / make a pizza ✓
4 you / play the guitar ✗ / sing ✗
5 they / skateboard ✓ / run very fast ✓

5 Complete the questions and short answers.
1 *Can you swim* (you/swim)?
   No, *I can't*.
2 _____ (David/sing) this song?
   Yes, _____ . He's very good.
3 _____ (the boys/act)?
   No, _____ !
4 _____ (Lisa/play) this game?
   No, _____ . She's really bad!
5 _____ (you/see) Mario?
   Yes, _____ . He's over there.

Speaking

6 Put the dialogue in the correct order. Then act it out in pairs.
a ☐ I'm not sure … I can't play very well.
b ☐ OK, cool. Let's do that.
c ☐ I agree. Any ideas?
d [1] Let's do something fun.
e ☐ No problem. I can teach you.
f ☐ We can play football.

83 Unit 5

BBC CULTURE — Young London

Hyde Park

Natural History Museum

The London Eye and the Thames

1 Do you know these places in London? What are they? What can you do there?

2 🔊 5.19 Listen and read. Match photos A–D with paragraphs 1–4.

Things to do at the weekend

London is a fun city. There are a lot of things young people can do. Here are some of them.

A
1 ☐ **Go to a museum**
How about the Natural History Museum? There are fun activities for teens: you can make dinosaur T-shirts, see a puppet show or be a scientist for a day!

B
2 ☐ **Workshops**
Some museums have workshops. You can draw or make things with your friends. At the Cartoon Museum, you can make your own comic!

C
3 ☐ **See a show**
London is famous for its musicals. There are many shows. You can sing and dance to the songs too!

D
4 ☐ **See the city**
You can see London from the top of the London Eye or from a boat on the Thames. You can run, play football, skateboard or have a picnic in Hyde Park.

activity (n) something you do because you enjoy it
workshop (n) a place where people meet to learn or improve a skill
comic (n) a magazine that tells a story with pictures

3 Read the text in Exercise 2 again. Choose the correct option.
Where can you …
1 skateboard?
on the London Eye / (in Hyde Park)
2 make a comic?
at a workshop / on the Thames
3 sing?
in the Natural History Museum / in a musical
4 go on a boat?
from the top of the London Eye / on the Thames
5 make a T-shirt?
at the Natural History Museum / at the Cartoon Museum

4 🔊 5.20 Listen and write where the people are. Choose from the places below.

a drawing workshop   a musical
a puppet show   the London Eye

1	the London Eye
2	
3	
4	

5 Work in pairs. What can teenagers do where you live? Make a list and compare with other students' lists. Whose list is the longest?

BBC ▶ Free-time activities

6 ▶ 29 Watch the video and answer the presenter's questions. Which activity is not in the video? Choose the correct answer.
   a boxing	b skateboarding	c swimming	d ice-skating

7 ▶ 29 Watch the video again. Mark the sentences T (true) or F (false). Use the information from the video, not what you know.
   1 You can ride a BMX bike in Rom Park.	T / F
   2 You can't skateboard in Rom Park.	T / F
   3 There are special hats for climbing.	T / F
   4 Boxing isn't a sport.	T / F
   5 Sports can help you make new friends.	T / F

8 Discuss in pairs. Which of the sports or activities in the video can you do? Which would you like to do?

PROJECT TIME

9 In pairs, make a promotional email about the fun things visitors can do in your area.

1 Take photos of the places or find them on the internet.

2 Write about places with fun activities for teenagers. Use these questions to help you.
   • What kind of places are they?
   • Where are they?
   • What can people do there?

3 Put the photos and text together on a digital document.

4 Email it to your classmates.

Fun things to do in ...*

This is …
It's in …
You can *do fun activities / skateboard / see a film there.*

*Add the name of the place where you live.

My day

6

VOCABULARY
Daily activities | Days of the week
Months | On the internet

GRAMMAR
Present Simple affirmative
Adverbs of frequency

MY DAY ...
FROM START
TO FINISH

6.1 Vocabulary

Daily activities

1 Which activities below do you do every day?

do (my) homework   go to bed   go to school   have lunch   watch TV

2 🔊 **6.1** Listen and repeat. Which activities from the Vocabulary box can you see in the pictures on page 86?

VOCABULARY ▶ **Daily activities**

do my homework   get up   go to bed
go to school   hang out with my friends
have a shower   have breakfast   have dinner
have lessons   have lunch   listen to music
tidy my room   watch TV

3 Choose the correct option.
1 *get* / *go* to bed
2 *have* / *get* up
3 *tidy* / *listen to* my room
4 *have* / *go* lessons
5 *watch* / *listen to* music
6 *take* / *watch* TV
7 *do* / *have* my homework
8 *take* / *hang* out with my friends.

4 Complete the phrases with the words below.

a shower   breakfast   dinner   lessons   ~~lunch~~

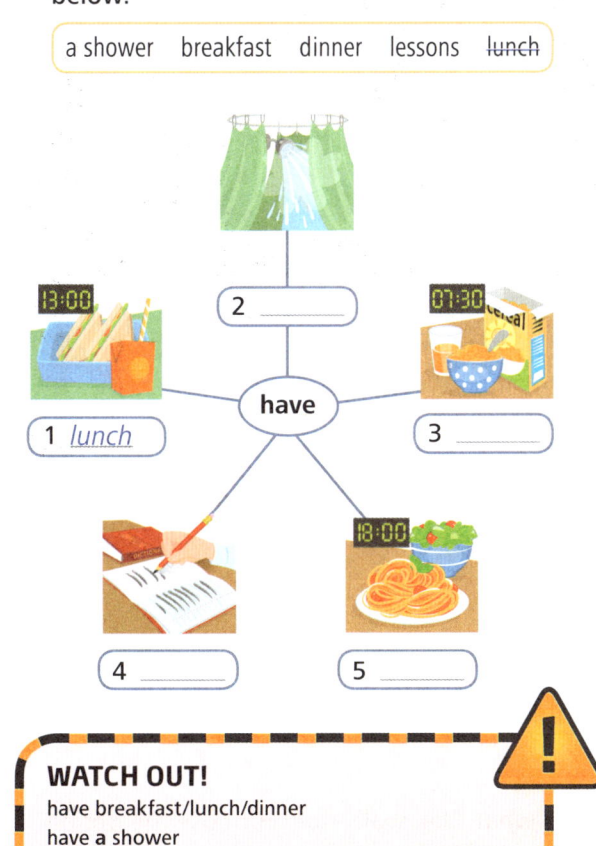

1 lunch
2 ___
3 ___
4 ___
5 ___

WATCH OUT!
have breakfast/lunch/dinner
have a shower
have lessons

5 🔊 **6.2** Listen and write six activities from the Vocabulary box in your notebook.
1 *watch TV*

6 Number the activities in the order you do them on a typical day. Then, in pairs, read your lists. Are they the same?
☐ have dinner   *1* get up
☐ have lessons   ☐ have breakfast
☐ go to school   ☐ go to bed
☐ do my homework   ☐ have lunch

7 Look at the photos. Write the activities.

1 *hang out with my friends*
2 ___ 
3 ___ 
4 ___ 
5 ___ 
6 ___ 

8 In pairs, play the board game on page 86.

1 Throw the dice.
2 Go forward.
3 If there is a picture on the square, say the activity.
   Correct answer: stay there.
   Wrong answer: go back two squares.
4 Go to the FINISH first to win!

YOUR WORLD

9 Put the daily activities in the Vocabulary box into groups.
☺ Activities I like: …
☹ Activities I don't like: …

I can talk about daily activities.   **87** Unit 6

6.2 Grammar
Present Simple affirmative

VIDEO ▶ **I LISTEN TO CLASSICAL MUSIC.**

1 Lucas asks Jen and Alex about their daily routine for a school survey.

2
Jen: I get up early. I get ready for school and I have breakfast.
Alex: Me too. Breakfast is very important. Jen makes pancakes!
Jen: Then we walk to school.
Alex: We're never late for school.

3
Jen: After school, we do our homework. In the evening, . . .
Alex: . . . I listen to classical music and Jen plays the piano.

4
Lucas: Come on, guys! Alex listens to classical music! Jen plays the piano! Seriously?
Jen: Oh, Alex! Lucas, this is what Alex really does . . .

1 ▶ 30 🔊 6.3 Watch the video. Then listen and read. Who makes breakfast? Choose the correct answer.
   a Lucas   b Alex   c Jen

2 Who does these things? Write *A* (Alex), *J* (Jen), or *A and J* (Alex and Jen).
   1 get up early — *A and J*
   2 make pancakes _____
   3 walk to school _____
   4 do homework _____
   5 listen to classical music _____
   6 play the piano _____

SOUNDS GOOD!   Me too. • Come on, guys! • Seriously?

3 🔊 6.4 Listen and repeat. Find these expressions in the story.

4 Guess what Alex really does. Choose the option that you think is correct.
   1 He gets up *early / late.*
   2 He has breakfast *at home / at school.*
   3 He plays *computer games / football.*

5 ▶ 31 🔊 6.5 Now watch or listen and check.

Unit 6 88

6 Study the Grammar box. Then watch.

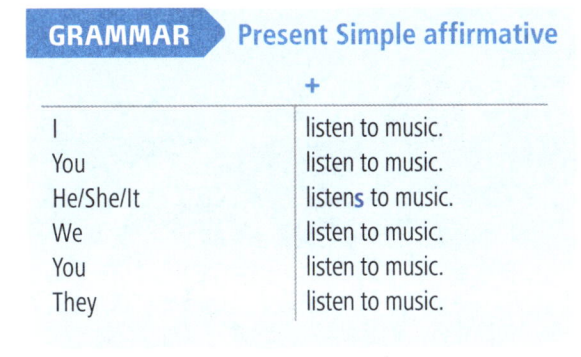

GRAMMAR	Present Simple affirmative
+	
I	listen to music.
You	listen to music.
He/She/It	listen**s** to music.
We	listen to music.
You	listen to music.
They	listen to music.

VIDEO ▶ **32 GET GRAMMAR!**

I *go* to bed early. Hammy *goes* to bed early too.

7 Choose the correct option.

I ¹*get* / *gets* up early. Alex ²*get* / *gets* up late. He ³*have* / *has* breakfast at school. I ⁴*have* / *has* breakfast at home.

Jen and I ⁵*walk* / *walks* to school. After school, we ⁶*do* / *does* our homework. In the evening, I ⁷*play* / *plays* computer games.

WATCH OUT!
get → gets   make → makes
watch → watches   go → goes
tidy → tidies   have → has

8 Read Lucas's blog. Complete the sentences with the Present Simple form of the verbs below.

~~get~~   get   go   hang   have   have   play   watch

LUCAS'S BLOG

My brother and I are very different. Victor ¹*gets* up early. I ²_____ up late. I ³_____ breakfast at home, but Victor ⁴_____ to the swimming pool, so he ⁵_____ breakfast at school. Before dinner, I ⁶_____ computer games and Victor ⁷_____ out with his friends. But we ⁸_____ football on TV together!

9 Tick (✓) the things that you do. Tell your partner. Then listen to your partner and tick (✓) the things he/she does.

	Me	Partner
1 I get up early.	☐	☐
2 I get up late.	☐	☐
3 I have breakfast at home.	☐	☐
4 I have breakfast at school.	☐	☐
5 I do my homework after school.	☐	☐
6 I hang out with my friends after school.	☐	☐
7 I watch TV after dinner.	☐	☐
8 I play computer games after dinner.	☐	☐

10 Look at Exercise 9. In your notebook, write what you and you partner do.

I get up early. Nicola gets up early too. After school, I …

YOUR WORLD

11 Play *Who is it?*

I play basketball after school.

It's Oliver! He plays basketball after school.

I can use the Present Simple in affirmative sentences.

6.3 Grammar
Adverbs of frequency

The Terrific Two – Dug's busy week

Kit: Dug, your garage is a mess! Can you tidy it, please?

Dug: Sorry, Kit. Today's Monday. On Mondays, I always go to the superhero gym.

Kit: How about Tuesday?

Dug: Tuesday isn't a good day. I have swimming lessons on Tuesday.

Kit: OK. Wednesday.

Dug: I usually have dinner with Uncle Roberto on Wednesday.

Kit: Thursday? Friday? Saturday?

Dug: I'm often busy on these days. On Thursday, I visit my parents. On Friday, I play football for the superhero team. And on Saturday, we always hang out with our friends.

Kit: How about Sunday?

Dug: But Sunday is my only free day!

Kit: Not this Sunday!

1 Look at the cartoon. Can you see Dug's football shirt? What colour is it?

2 🔊 6.6 Listen and read. Which is Dug's free day?

3 Three activities from Dug's busy week are not in the cartoon. Which activities are they?

4 Correct the sentences.
1. Dug's ~~kitchen~~ is a mess. *garage*
2. Dug has singing lessons. _____
3. Dug has lunch with Uncle Roberto. _____
4. Dug visits his granny and grandad. _____
5. Dug plays basketball for the superhero team. _____

5 Study the Grammar box. Then watch.

> **GRAMMAR** — Adverbs of frequency
>
> ●●●●● We **always** hang out with our friends.
> ●●●●○ He **usually** goes to the gym.
> ●●●○○ I **often** visit my granny.
> ●●○○○ She **sometimes** has dinner with us.
> ○○○○○ They **never** get up late.
>
> | Adverb + verb | Adverb + the verb *to be* |
> |---|---|
> | I **always** have breakfast. | I am **always** happy. |
> | They **never** get up late. | They are **never** late. |

VIDEO ▶ 33 GET GRAMMAR!

We often watch DVDs.
And we always eat popcorn.

6 In your notebook, write the sentences with the adverb in the correct place.
1 Dug has dinner with Kit. — usually
   Dug usually has dinner with Kit.
2 He plays computer games. — sometimes
3 He is at home on Tuesday. — never
4 He listens to music. — often
5 He is late for breakfast. — always

7 In your notebook, write about Kit's sisters, Lulu and Flo. Use the adverbs in the Grammar box.

1 Lulu and Flo / go to the cinema on Friday   ●●●○○
   Lulu and Flo often go to the cinema on Friday.
2 Lulu and Flo / hang out with Kit and Dug.   ●●○○○
3 Lulu / go to bed early   ●●●●○
4 Flo / play computer games   ○○○○○
5 they / be late for school   ●●○○○
6 they / do their homework before dinner   ●●●●●

8 🔊 6.7 Listen and repeat.

> **VOCABULARY** — Days of the week
>
> Monday Tuesday Wednesday Thursday
> Friday Saturday Sunday

9 Read the clues and write the days.
1 / 3 is a Monday.
1 / 6 is a Tuesday.
1 / 8 is a Sunday.
1 / 10 is a Wednesday.

1 _____ 17/3
2 _____ 26/6
3 _____ 6/8
4 _____ 30/10

10 Complete the words. In pairs, say when Kit does these activities. Which day is missing?
1 watch a film   F _r_ _i_ day
2 get up late   S _ _ _ day
3 cook dinner   W _ _ _ _ _ day
4 tidy her house   S _ _ day
5 have a tennis lesson M _ _ day
6 go to the gym   T _ _ _ day

Kit watches a film on Friday.

YOUR WORLD

11 In your notebook, write sentences that are true for you.
1 always
   I always watch TV on Saturday.
2 sometimes
3 often
4 usually
5 never

12 Work in pairs. Student A, say one true and one false sentence about the things you do. Student B, spot the false sentence. Then change roles and have the conversation again.
A: I never get up late. I often cook.
B: True, false!
A: Correct!

I can use adverbs of frequency.

6.4 Speaking
Telling the time

VIDEO ▶ **THE FILM STARTS AT FOUR O'CLOCK.**

1 Alex and Lian want to go to the cinema.

Lian: What time is it?
Alex: It's **a quarter to four**. (1)
Lian: What time is the film?
Alex: It's at **four o'clock**. (2)
Lian: It's too late now.
Alex: Wait, the film is on again at **half past four**. (3)
Lian: That's better. Let's go.

2 At the cinema.

Lian: There isn't a film at half past four.
Alex: But it says here there is a film at half past four on Fridays. Oh!
Lian: Exactly! Today's Saturday.

1 Find the times 1–3 in the story. Match them with clocks a–c.
a ☐   b ☐   c ☐

2 ▶ 34 🔊 6.8 Watch the video. Then listen and read. Why isn't there a film at half past four?

3 🔊 6.9 Listen and repeat.

SPEAKING — Telling the time

A: **What time is it?**
B: **It's** four **o'clock**.

A: **What time is the** film/match?
B: **It's at** ten **(minutes) past** four.
    (a) **quarter past** four.
    half past four.
    (a) **quarter to** five.
    ten **(minutes) to** five.

4 Complete the times. Then ask and answer in pairs.
1 05:40 It's twenty _to_ six.
2 02:30 It's _____ past two.
3 10:15 It's a quarter _____ ten.
4 03:00 It's three _____.
5 05:10 It's ten past _____.
6 07:45 It's a quarter _____ eight.

A: What time is it?
B: It's twenty to six.

5 In pairs, make dialogues. Then act them out in class.
1 A: time / the football match?   B: 12:15
   What time is the football match?
   A: time / now?   B: 11:55
2 A: time?   B: 5:40
   A: time / the party?   B: 6:00

YOUR WORLD

6 Play *What time is it?* as a class. Ask and answer.
A: What time is it?
B: It's one o'clock. What time is it?
C: It's five past one. What time is it?
D: It's …

Unit 6   I can tell the time.

6.5 Reading and Vocabulary
Interview with a traveller

1 Look at the photos and read the first part of the text. Why is this family special?

2 🔊 6.10 Read and listen to the rest of the text. Choose the correct option.
1. Réka lives in *Australia* / *different countries*.
2. Réka has got a *brother* / *sister*.
3. Réka *has got* / *hasn't got* a school.
4. Réka hangs out with her friends *in different places* / *online*.
5. 'Dreamtime Traveler' is Réka's *book* / *blog*.
6. Réka's life *is* / *isn't* boring.

3 Read the text again and answer the questions.
1. Who is Lalika?
   He's Réka's brother.
2. Who are Réka's teachers?
3. Has Réka got a best friend?
4. What are her two favourite activities?
5. Réka hasn't got a pet. Why?
6. What does Réka watch?

4 In pairs, talk about what you like most about Réka's life.

5 🔊 6.11 Listen and repeat. Match five months from the Vocabulary box with photos 1–5.

> **VOCABULARY** ▸ **Months**
>
> January   February   March   April   May
> June   July   August   September   October
> November   December

6 Imagine you travel to different countries, like Réka. Plan your journey for a year. Tell the class about your plan.

Month	Country
January and February	Australia

In January and in February, I'm in Australia. In March, I'm in …

---

by Burak Yilmaz *September 2016*

A DAY WITH ... DREAMTIME TRAVELER!

1. Australia – January 2016
2. Machu Picchu – March 2013
3. Nazca – March 2013
4. Cappadocia, Turkey – October 2014
5. Paris, France – August 2015

Réka Kaponay is from Australia, but she lives in different countries! She travels with her parents and brother, Lalika. Today she tells us about her life.

Where's your school?

I haven't got a school! My teachers are my parents and the people we visit.

Who are your friends?

I've got friends in a lot of countries. We hang out online. I haven't got a best friend.

Have you got a pet?

No! I love animals, but I can't have a pet. We are always in different places.

What are your favourite hobbies?

Reading and writing. I read a lot and I write my own books. I've got a blog too – Dreamtime Traveler. But I also watch TV and films, like all teenagers, and I love walking and swimming.

Do you like your life?

Yes, I love every day! It's never boring!

I can understand a text about a teenage life.

6.6 Listening and Writing
A typical weekend

1 Tick (✓) the activities you do at the weekend. In pairs, compare your answers.
1. ☐ tidy my room
2. ☐ play football
3. ☐ ride my bike
4. ☐ listen to music
5. ☐ watch TV
6. ☐ sing
7. ☐ play computer games
8. ☐ do my homework
9. ☐ have lunch with my family

2 🔊 **6.12** Listen and match people 1–3 with pictures A–D. There is one extra picture.
1. Brian _____ 2. Ben _____ 3. Anna _____

3 🔊 **6.13** Listen to Ben talking about his weekend. Complete the sentences with a word you hear.
1. Ben _usually_ gets up at seven o'clock on Saturday.
2. Ben tidies his room after _____ .
3. Ben goes to bed at _____ o'clock on Saturday.
4. Ben _____ does his homework after breakfast on Sunday.
5. Ben and his best friend play the _____ on Sunday.

4 Work in groups. Talk about what you usually do at the weekend. Then tell your class about a student in your group. Can they guess who it is?

5 Read Lian's blog. Which is her favourite day? Choose the correct answer.
a Saturday b Sunday

MY WEEKEND

I usually get up at eight o'clock on Saturdays. After breakfast, I skateboard with my friends. I love my skateboard and I love Saturdays! Before dinner, I watch TV or play computer games.

I get up at nine o'clock on Sundays. Before lunch, I tidy my room and I do my homework. I always have lunch with my family. After lunch, I often draw or listen to music.

6 Study the Writing box. Find *before* and *after* in Lian's blog.

WRITING | *before, after*

tidy my room — lunch — play football

Before lunch, I tidy my room. I tidy my room **before** lunch.
After lunch, I play football. I play football **after** lunch.

WRITING TIME

7 Write about your typical weekend. Use *before* and *after*.

1 Find ideas
Make a list of what you do.
Saturday: get up late, help Mum, …
Sunday: do my homework, …

2 Draft
Write a paragraph about Saturday.
I usually get up at … o'clock on Saturday.
I have a shower and I have breakfast.
After breakfast, I …
Write a paragraph about Sunday.
I always … on Sunday. Before lunch, I …

3 Check and write
Check *before* and *after* and write the final version of your text.

I can understand and write short texts about a typical weekend.

6.7 CLIL: Technology
The internet

1 🔊 6.14 Listen and repeat. Match the phrases in the Vocabulary box with photos 1–6.

VOCABULARY — **On the internet**

chat online   email someone   get help with homework
have a video call   read/write a blog   watch videos online

1 _____   2 _____   3 _____

4 _____   5 _____   6 _____

2 Read the online posts. Complete them with six words from the Vocabulary box.

The internet and me!

chocolatecookie My best friend lives in the USA now. We are in different time zones: London time is Los Angeles time + 8 hours. When it's five o'clock in the morning in LA, it's one o'clock in the afternoon in London, so we only ¹*chat* online on weekdays. But we always have a video ² _____ on Saturday or Sunday.

FierceTed I love the internet! I get help with my ³ _____. I play games online with my friends. We can play from our homes. I also watch ⁴ _____ online.

Cherry I write *Classmates*. It's a fun ⁵ _____ with stories and cartoons about school life. A lot of kids read it and they ⁶ _____ me their stories. I usually post them on my blog.

3 Read the posts again. Answer the questions.
1 When it's two o'clock in London, what time is it in Los Angeles?
   It's ten o'clock.
2 Which days of the week are 'weekdays'? Guess.
3 When *FierceTed* plays games with his friends, are they all in the same room?
4 What is the name of *Cherry*'s blog?

4 Find one more thing you can do on the internet in one of the posts. Then add your own ideas. Ask your teacher or find the words you need online!
More things I can do on the internet:
1 _____
2 _____
3 _____

YOUR WORLD

5 Write a post for *The internet and me!* about you. Create an online name first!

[_____] I usually …

I can describe things I can do on the internet.   **95** Unit 6

Vocabulary Activator

WORDLIST 🔊 6.15

Daily activities
do my homework
get up (v)
go to bed
go to school
hang out with my friends
have a shower
have breakfast
have dinner
have lessons
have lunch
listen to music
tidy my room
watch TV

Days of the week
Monday (n)
Tuesday (n)
Wednesday (n)
Thursday (n)
Friday (n)
Saturday (n)
Sunday (n)

Months
January (n)
February (n)
March (n)
April (n)
May (n)
June (n)
July (n)
August (n)
September (n)
October (n)
November (n)
December (n)

On the internet
chat online
email someone
get help with homework
have a video call
read/write a blog
watch videos online

Extra words
animal (n)

busy (adj)
busy week
cartoon (n)
classical music (n)
Come on, guys!
daily routine
early (adv)
every (determiner)
free day
get ready
grandparent (n)
gym (n)
hour (n)
How about …?
in the evening
late (adv)
lesson (n)
life (n)
live (v)
love (v)
Me too.
meet (v)

mess (n)
never (adv)
often (adv)
online (adv)
pancake (n)
really (adv)
school survey
Seriously?
swimming (n)
team (n)
teenager (n)
That's better.
The film is on again at …
too late
travel (v)
visit (v)
walk (v)
walking (n)
weekday (n)
writing (n)

1 Complete the sentences with the Present Simple form of verbs from the wordlist.
1 Jack usually *tidies* the kitchen after breakfast.
2 We always _____ out with our friends on Saturday.
3 She _____ to music in her room.
4 I never _____ up late on weekdays.
5 My brother _____ his homework on Friday.
6 They often _____ TV in the evening.
7 Dad sometimes _____ a shower after dinner.
8 We _____ lessons on Monday and Thursday.
9 Paul often _____ to bed at nine o'clock.
10 You usually _____ lunch at school.

2 Write the dates in full.
1 Mon. 6/7 — *Monday, 6 July*
2 Wed. 25/3 — _____
3 Sun. 10/2 — _____
4 Fri. 8/8 — _____
5 Sat. 29/1 — _____
6 Tues. 12/5 — _____
7 Thurs. 17/11 — _____
8 Mon. 22/10 — _____
9 Wed. 14/4 — _____
10 Sat. 1/6 — _____
11 Tue. 9/9 — _____
12 Thurs. 13/12 — _____

3 Match 1–6 with a–f. Then choose three phrases and write sentences.

1	email	a	online
2	chat	b	a blog
3	get	c	videos online
4	write	d	a video call
5	have	e	a friend
6	watch	f	help with homework

On Saturdays, my sister watches videos online with her friends.

4 🔊 6.16 **PRONUNCIATION** /s/, /z/ or /ɪz/
Listen and repeat.
Kate get**s** up late and ha**s** breakfast fast,
She watch**es** a film and run**s** for the bus!

Unit 6

Revision

Vocabulary

1 Complete the phrases with the words below. There is one extra word.

> friends   go to   have   ~~homework~~   listen to
> my room   school   up   watch

1 do my *homework*
2 get _____
3 _____ TV
4 go to _____
5 _____ bed
6 _____ music
7 tidy _____
8 hang out with my _____

The extra word is _____.

2 Write three phrases with the extra word from Exercise 1. Do you know any more phrases with this word?

1 _____ a sh _ _ _ r
2 _____ b _ _ k _ _ _ t
3 _____ l _ ss _ _ s

3 Find the days of the week. In pairs, say them. Which day is missing?

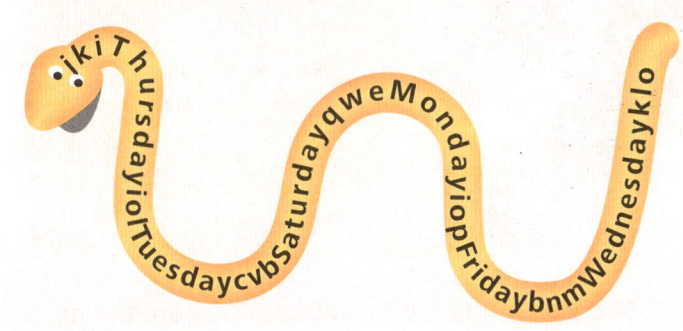

4 Answer the questions. Then tell a friend.
1 Which month is your birthday? _____
2 Which month is before January? _____
3 Which month is after February? _____
4 Which month is before May? _____

5 Choose the correct option.

1 email a friend / listen to music
2 get help with homework / watch videos online 
3 play computer games / write a blog 
4 have a video call / chat online 

Grammar

6 Complete the text with the Present Simple form of the verbs below.

> get (x3)   go   hang   have (x3)   listen

I ¹*get* up at half past seven, but my parents ² _____ up at seven o'clock. My sister, Kate, ³ _____ up late every day! We ⁴ _____ breakfast together. After breakfast, I ⁵ _____ to school with Kate. We go on the bus. Kate ⁶ _____ to music and I ⁷ _____ out with my friends. We ⁸ _____ lessons and we ⁹ _____ lunch at one o'clock.

7 In your notebook, write sentences that are true for you.
1 My brother/sister *always gets up late*. (always)
2 My parents _____. (usually)
3 My best friend _____. (often)
4 My granny and grandad _____. (sometimes)
5 My teacher _____. (never)
6 I _____. (always)

Speaking

8 Choose the correct option.

1 06:35 It's twenty-five to six / *seven*.
2 12:30 It's *a quarter* / half past twelve.
3 06:10 It's *ten past six* / six past ten.
4 04:00 It's four *past* / o'clock.
5 09:45 It's a quarter to *ten* / nine.
6 01:50 It's *fifty past one* / ten to two.

9 Match 1–3 with a–c and make two dialogues.

Dialogue 1
1 ☐ What time is it?   a OK!
2 ☐ What time is the show?   b It's five to two.
3 ☐ Let's watch it.   c At two o'clock.

Dialogue 2
1 ☐ When is the match?   a It's a quarter to eleven.
2 ☐ What time is it now?   b Yes, let's go!
3 ☐ Let's walk fast then!   c It's at eleven o'clock.

SET FOR LIFE

Give things a new life!

What can we do with old or broken things?

We can recycle some things, but we can't recycle all of them.

The things we can't recycle usually go to a landfill. They stay there for a long, long time. Landfills use a lot of space and they are not good for the environment.

A landfill

We use a lot of energy to make new things like mobile phones or clothes. This is bad for the environment too.

How can we help?

Repair things! ✓

Use things in a different way ✓

Save energy!
Save space!
Save the environment!

---

1 What do you usually do with things 1–4? Choose a, b or c.
 a Throw them away.
 b Repair them.
 c Recycle them.

1
2
3
4

2 Read the poster above. Answer the questions.
 1 What happens to the things we can't recycle?
 2 Why is it good to repair broken things or use them in a different way?

3 🔊 6.17 Listen to Mike and Suzie. They are talking about repairing things. Choose the correct option.

SHOW YOU CARE: REPAIR!

Join our repair workshops!

When? ¹ *Sunday /(Saturday)* mornings at ² *11 a.m. / 1 p.m.*
Where? Bay Road Centre

Bring your ³ *broken / new* things.
Our team can ⁴ *recycle / repair* them for you.
We can teach you how to repair them too!

Bring your old things and give them a new life! There are a lot of fun projects with the things we can't fix.
Make a cat bed with old ⁵ *clothes / bags*!

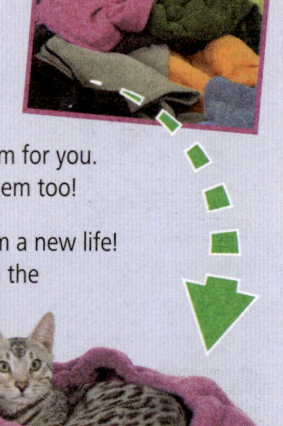

I can repair things or use them again.

Repair or use again

4 🔊 **6.18** Listen to Mike and Suzie again. Choose the correct option.

> **What we do in our workshop:**
> We repair slow ¹ *phones / (computers)*.
> We show you how to paint your ² *desks / chairs*. You can make them look ³ *new / cool*!
> We ⁴ *throw away / use* things we can't repair.

5 In pairs, look at photos A–D. What are the things? What are they made from? Look up any words you need.

A
B
C
D

USEFUL TIPS

- It is not good for the environment to throw away things.
- Learn how to repair broken things.
- Take parts from a broken thing and make something new.
- Use things in a different way.
- Give the things you no longer want to other people.

SET FOR LIFE

6 Make a new object from something old or broken. Make a digital presentation of the process. Follow these steps.

1. Find an old or broken thing. Make a list of things you can do with it or with parts of it.
2. Choose an idea and do your project. Take photos of every step.
3. Make a digital presentation with the photos.
4. Show your presentation to the class.

Progress Check Units 1–6

Vocabulary and Grammar

1 Choose the correct answer.
1 This day is after Wednesday and before Friday.
 a Tuesday b Saturday c Thursday
2 You _____ to music.
 a play b listen c hear
3 You wear them on your feet. They're good for running.
 a shoes b trainers c trousers
4 You have this meal before you go to school.
 a dinner b lunch c breakfast
5 This month has 31 days.
 a February b October c June
6 You do this with a pen and a notebook.
 a write b read c speak

2 Complete the text with one word in each gap.

My bedroom is small. I've ¹ *got* a big bed, but I ² _____ got a desk. Our house has got a big living room. ³ _____ are two desks in it: one for my brother and one for me. I usually ⁴ _____ my homework after school. My brother ⁵ _____ football after school, so he ⁶ _____ his homework before dinner. We usually have dinner at half ⁷ _____ six. After dinner, I ⁸ _____ computer games and my brother ⁹ _____ videos online. We always ¹⁰ _____ to bed early on weekdays.

Speaking

3 Look at the pictures. Match sentences a–h with pictures 1–6. There are two extra sentences.

a No, it isn't a good idea. _____
b The film's at a quarter to five. _____
c Let's do something fun! _____
d Let's go skateboarding! _____
e Swimming? I'm not sure. _____
f Swimming? Great idea! _____
g We can ride our bikes! _____
h What time is it? _____

4 In pairs, ask and answer the questions.
1 What's your favourite month?
2 Who can sing in your family?
3 What cool things can you do?
4 Have you got a book in English?

Reading

5 In pairs, talk about what you and your family can and can't do.

A: *I can play the guitar.*
B: *My brother can't dance!*

6 Read the ad. What is it about? Choose the correct answer.
   a   a talent contest   b   a London show

7 Read the ad again. Answer the questions.
   1 Who is Meryl? *She's a new star.*
   2 What can she do? _____
   3 How many prizes are there? _____
   4 When is the contest? _____
   5 Where is it? _____
   6 Can dogs come? _____

Listening

8 🔊 6.19 Listen and tick (✓) the correct answer.
   1 What can Grace do?
      a ☐   b ☐   c ☐
   2 What club is on Thursday?
      a ☐   b ☐   c ☐
   3 What time is the film?
      a ☐   b ☐   c ☐
      08:15   07:35   07:45
   4 Where is Jill?
      a ☐   b ☐   c ☐
   5 What can Uncle Jack do?
      a ☐   b ☐   c ☐

New Stars!

You can be a star too!

This is Meryl. She's a new star! She sings and plays the guitar in a rock band. She can dance too. What can you do? Show us! We've got special prizes.

Prize 1 You can be on TV!
Prize 2 Meet a famous band!
Prize 3 Go to a London show!

When: Saturday at 8 o'clock
Where: Town Theatre
Your family and friends can come too!
We're sorry, but no dogs.

Writing

9 Complete Dan's blog with the words below. There are two extra words.

| after | breakfast | can | garden | get | hang | have |
| ~~house~~ | listen | room | the | usually | | |

I'm at my cousin Julie's ¹*house* this week. It's in Richmond. It isn't very big, but it's got a fantastic ²_____! My uncle and aunt ³_____ up at half past six. I get up at seven and have ⁴_____ with them and Julie. ⁵_____ breakfast, I go to bed again – it's the holidays! Then I tidy my ⁶_____. Julie and I ⁷_____ do sports after lunch. Julie ⁸_____ skateboard really well. She's my new teacher! We often ⁹_____ out with Julie's friends before dinner. Before bed, we ¹⁰_____ to music or watch TV.

10 You are at a friend's house for the holidays. Write 40–50 words about what you do. Use these questions to help you.
   1 Where is your friend's house?
   2 What time do you get up?
   3 What do you do before and after lunch?
   4 What do you do in the evening?

I'm at my friend's house this week. It's in … I get up at … I have breakfast with … Before lunch, I/ we … After lunch, I/we … In the evening I/we …

VOCABULARY
Wild animals | Pets | Adjectives | Where animals live

GRAMMAR
Present Simple negative | Present Simple questions and short answers

Animals
7

7.1 Vocabulary
Wild animals

1 Find the animals below in photos A–H. There is one extra photo.

crocodile   elephant   giraffe   kangaroo   lion   monkey   tiger

2 🔊 **7.1** Listen and repeat. What is the name of the animal in the extra photo on page 102?

VOCABULARY — Wild animals

bird butterfly crocodile elephant fish
fly frog giraffe kangaroo lion monkey
snake spider tiger whale

3 Look at photos 1–7 and complete the words. Use the Vocabulary box to help you.

1 b u _t_ _t_ e r _f_ l y
2 b __ r __
3 __ l y
4 s __ a k __
5 __ p i d __ __
6 f __ __ g
7 __ i s __

4 🔊 **7.2** Listen to the animal sounds. Number the animals. Then check your answers in pairs.
a ☐ bird
b ☐ elephant
c ☐ frog
d [1] lion
e ☐ monkey
f ☐ snake

5 Read the sentences and choose the correct option.

1 I can fly!
spider / (bird)

2 I can swim!
whale / butterfly

3 I'm very tall!
frog / giraffe

4 I can't jump!
kangaroo / elephant

5 I've got big teeth!
crocodile / fly

6 I haven't got arms and legs.
snake / monkey

6 The names of the animals are mixed up. Write the correct names.

1 ti | on
2 kanga | fly
3 butter | dile
4 croco | roo
5 li | key
6 mon | ger

1 _tiger_
2 _____
3 _____
4 _____
5 _____
6 _____

YOUR WORLD

7 Draw three fantasy animals. In pairs, look at the animals and give them a name.
A: It's a giraffe and a bird.
B: It's a 'giraffird'!
A: Or a 'biraffe'!

I can talk about wild animals.

7.2 Grammar
Present Simple negative

VIDEO ▶ I DON'T LIKE CATS!

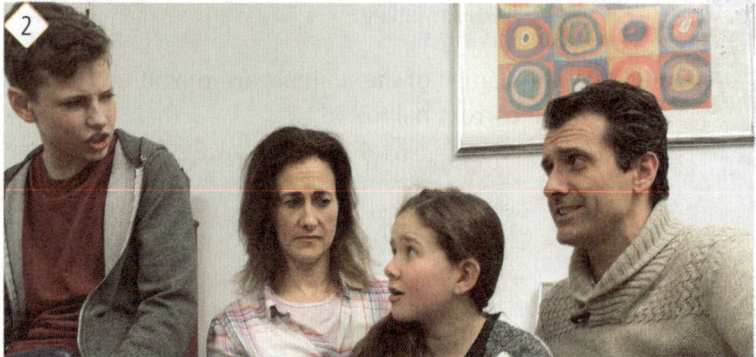

1
Alex: Mum? I want a dog like this! Please?
Mum: Aww … I like dogs, but they are hard work, Alex.
Alex: I don't mind!

2
Mum: Can you get up early and take it for a walk? Every day?
Jen: Poor dog! Alex doesn't get up before twelve o'clock at the weekend.
Dad: Big dogs eat a lot.
Alex: But it's small! It doesn't eat a lot.
Dad: Because it's a puppy! These dogs are usually very big!
Alex: Oh, all right.

3
Jen: How about a cat? People don't take cats for a walk.
Alex: I don't like cats! And I'm allergic!
Dad: Look, these are perfect for you! They don't eat a lot and you are not allergic to them.

---

1 ▶ 35 🔊 7.3 Watch the video. Then listen and read. Find a word that means 'baby dog'.

SOUNDS GOOD! I don't mind! • Poor (dog)! • Oh, all right!

2 Read the sentences. Mark them T (true) or F (false).
1 Alex's mum doesn't like dogs. T / F
2 Alex gets up late at the weekend. T / F
3 Dad thinks small dogs eat a lot. T / F
4 The puppy in Alex's photo is very big. T / F
5 A cat isn't a good pet for Alex. T / F

3 🔊 7.4 Listen and repeat. Find these expressions in the story. How do you say them in your language?

4 Guess what kind of pet is good for Alex in Dad's opinion.

5 ▶ 36 🔊 7.5 Now watch or listen and check.

Unit 7

6 Study the Grammar box. Then watch.

GRAMMAR	Present Simple negative
I	don't (do not) get up early.
You	don't (do not) get up early.
He/She/It	doesn't (does not) get up early.
We	don't (do not) get up early.
You	don't (do not) get up early.
They	don't (do not) get up early.

VIDEO ▶ 37 GET GRAMMAR!

I don't go to school.

7 🔊 7.3 🔊 7.5 Choose the correct option. Then listen again and check.
1 Alex *wants* / *doesn't want* a cat.
2 Small dogs *eat* / *don't eat* a lot.
3 Alex's mum *likes* / *doesn't like* the puppy in the photo.
4 Alex *gets up* / *doesn't get up* before twelve o'clock at the weekend.
5 People *take* / *don't take* cats for a morning walk.
6 Alex *wants* / *doesn't want* a goldfish.

8 Complete what Alex says with *don't* or *doesn't*.

1 On weekdays, Jen and I go to school, but we *don't* go to school at the weekend.

2 At the weekend, Lucas plays computer games, but he _____ play computer games on weekdays.

3 On weekdays, Jen gets up early, but she _____ get up early at the weekend.

9 In pairs, talk about what you do and don't do at the weekend.
I don't go to school at the weekend.

10 🔊 7.6 Listen and repeat. Match the words in the Vocabulary box with pictures 1–8.

VOCABULARY	Pets

cat   dog   goldfish   hamster
iguana   parrot   rabbit   tortoise

1 _____   2 _____   3 _____   4 _____

5 _____   6 _____   7 _____   8 _____

11 Which pet is good for these people?
Student A, read 1–3. Then listen to Student B and decide. Student B, go to page 142 to help Student A. Student A, choose the correct option.
1 Alex: *goldfish* / *dog*
2 Lucas: *parrot* / *hamster*
3 Lian: *iguana* / *rabbit*
A: A goldfish or a dog for Alex?
B: Alex wants to play with his pet.
A: A dog is a good pet for Alex, then.
Student B, read 4–6. Then listen to Student A and decide. Student A, go to page 142 to help Student B. Student B, choose the correct option.
4 Granny: *dog* / *hamster*
5 Aunt Megan: *tortoise* / *parrot*
6 Jen's friend, Emma: *goldfish* / *big dog*

4 I hang out with my friends at the weekend, but I _____ hang out with them on weekdays.

5 On weekdays, Lian does homework, but she _____ do homework at the weekend.

6 At the weekend, we watch films on TV, but we _____ watch TV on weekdays.

I can use the negative form of the Present Simple and talk about pets.

7.3 Grammar

Present Simple questions and short answers

The Terrific Two – Superdug's interview

1 A reporter from *Superhero* magazine is at Dug's house.

Reporter: Superdug, what do you do to relax?
Superdug: I play computer games with Kit.
Reporter: Does Superdug always win, Kit?
Kit: No, he doesn't.
Superdug: Kit is a very good player. I'm not.

2

Reporter: That's interesting! Do you speak any foreign languages, Superdug?
Superdug: No, I don't, but Kit speaks five languages. She can speak Chinese!
Kit: But Superdug plays the piano!

3

Reporter: Does he have piano lessons?
Kit: Yes, he does.
Superdug: Kit is my piano teacher.
Reporter: Do you sing, Superdug?
Superdug: Oh, no, I don't! I can't sing at all! Kit is a very good singer!

4

Reporter: Do you and Kit work together
Superdug: Yes, we do. She helps me with my work.
Reporter: OK. Thank you.

5 A week later …

Superdug: Eh? Superdug? No. Here's Superkit!
Kit: Oh …

1 Look at the cartoon. In what language is Kit's magazine?

2 🔊 7.7 Listen and read. Who is Superdug's piano teacher?

3 Read the sentences. Choose the correct option.
1 Superdug *watches TV* / *plays computer games* to relax.
2 Superdug *sometimes* / *always* wins computer games.
3 Kit *speaks* / *doesn't speak* foreign languages.
4 Superdug *is* / *isn't* a good piano player.
5 Kit *sings* / *doesn't sing* well.

Unit 7 106

4 Study the Grammar box. Then watch.

GRAMMAR — Present Simple questions and short answers

?	Short answers
Do I sing?	Yes, I do. / No, I don't.
Do you sing?	Yes, you do. / No, you don't.
Does he/she/it sing?	Yes, he/she/it does. / No, he/she/it doesn't.
Do we sing?	Yes, we do. / No, we don't.
Do you sing?	Yes, you do. / No, you don't.
Do they sing?	Yes, they do. / No, they don't.
What do you do to relax?	I play computer games.

VIDEO 38 GET GRAMMAR!

Does Max watch DVDs to relax?
Yes, he does.

5 Complete the reporter's other questions to Superdug with *do* or *does*.
1 *Do* you know Superman? (✗)
2 _____ you hang out with friends? (✓)
3 _____ Kit help you? (✓)
4 _____ you go to the gym? (✓)
5 _____ you and Kit go ice-skating? (✗)
6 _____ Kit teach music at a school? (✗)

6 In your notebook, write Superdug's answers to the questions in Exercise 5.
1 *No, I don't.*

7 Work in pairs. Student A, pretend you are the reporter. Student B, pretend you are Superdug. Role play the questions and answers in Exercises 5 and 6. Then change roles and have the conversation again.
A: *Do you know Superman?*
B: *No, I don't.*

8 In your notebook, write questions.
1 you / play the guitar?
   Do you play the guitar?
2 you / listen to pop music?
3 Superdug / eat superhero food?
4 Superdug / watch TV?
5 you and Superdug / hang out every day?
6 Superdug / have swimming lessons?

9 🔊 7.8 Listen to Kit's answers to the questions in Exercise 8. Write them in your notebook.
1 *No, I don't.*

10 Play a game. Complete the questions. In pairs, ask the questions and mime the answers. You get one point for each correct guess.
1 What *do you do* (do) to relax?
2 What _____ (have) for breakfast?
3 Where _____ (do) your homework?
4 What _____ (do) after school?
5 What _____ (do) on Friday after dinner?
6 Where _____ (hang out) with your friends?

A: *What do you do to relax?*
B: *(mimes the answer)*
A: *I know! You play the guitar!*

YOUR WORLD

11 🔊 7.9 🔊 7.10 Go to page 142. Listen and sing the Questions Song.

I can ask and answer questions in the Present Simple.

7.4 Speaking
Buying a ticket

VIDEO ▶ ONE TICKET, PLEASE.

Dad: Get a ticket, Lucas. Jen and I have got passes.
Attendant: Can I help you?
Lucas: Can I have one ticket to the zoo, please?
Attendant: That's eighteen pounds fifty, please.
Lucas: Here you are.
Attendant: Thank you. Here's your ticket.
Would you like a guide?
Lucas: No, thanks. I've got all the information on my phone. Where do we start?
Jen: At the café. I'm so hungry I could eat a horse!
Lucas: Shh! We're at the zoo.

1 ▶ 39 ◉ 7.11 Watch the video. Then listen and read. Why doesn't Lucas need a guide?

2 ◉ 7.12 Listen and repeat.

> **SPEAKING** Buying a ticket
>
> A: Can I help you?
> B: Can I have *one ticket/two tickets to the zoo*, please?
> A: That's *eighteen pounds fifty*.
> B: Here you are.
> A: Here's your ticket./Here are your tickets.
> B: Thanks.

3 ◉ 7.13 Put the dialogue in order. Then listen and check.
a ☐ Thanks.
b ☐ Here are your tickets.
c ☐ Can I have three tickets to the aquarium, please?
d ☐ Here you are.
e ☐ That's twelve pounds sixty, please.
f ☐ 1 Can I help you?

> ⚠️ **WATCH OUT!**
> £ = pound
> £4.20 = four (pounds) twenty

4 How much are the tickets?

ZOO £18.50
MUSEUM £8.20
CINEMA £9.10
CONCERT £19.15

1 *eighteen pounds fifty*
2 _____
3 _____
4 _____

5 In pairs, role play buying tickets to the museum.
A: help / you?   B: three tickets
   Can I help you?
A: £13.20   B: here
A: your tickets B: thanks

6 In pairs, role play three more dialogues. Use the tickets in Exercise 4 and the phrases in the Speaking box.

Unit 7   108   I can buy a ticket.

7.5 Reading and Vocabulary
Amazing animals

1 In your notebook, write names of animals which …
  a swim very well.   b eat a lot.   c can sing.

2 🔊 7.14 Read and listen to the texts from a web page about amazing animals. Match texts 1–3 with photos A–C.

Amazing animals!

A — an elephant
B — a giraffe
C — a humpback whale

1 ☐ These animals are very fast. They can run at 55 kilometres an hour! They only sleep one or two hours every night. They've got cute faces. They don't drink much water, but they like eating. They can eat leaves from tall trees. They eat 45 kilos of food every day!

2 ☐ These animals are big, but they can run very fast. They love water and they can swim too. They love their families. They are very clever and friendly, but sometimes they can be dangerous! They eat plants. They eat up to 270 kilos of food and they drink about 75 litres of water every day!

3 ☐ These animals eat a lot of very small fish and they are very strong. They can jump out of the water. They like having fun! They can sing and they 'write' different songs! Some people think they are ugly, but other people think they are cute.

3 Read the texts again and complete the table.

	giraffes	elephants	humpback whales
What do they eat/drink?	leaves, …		
What can they do?			jump, …
What do they like/love?			

4 🔊 7.15 Listen and repeat. Match the words in the Vocabulary box with pictures 1–6.

VOCABULARY Adjectives

cute   dangerous   fast   slow
strong   ugly

1 _____   2 _____
3 _____   4 _____
5 _____   6 _____

5 Read the texts in Exercise 2 again. Find and write the adjectives that describe each animal in your notebook.
giraffe: fast, …

6 🔊 7.16 Listen to two children. What animals do they talk about?
Speaker 1: _____
Speaker 2: _____

YOUR WORLD

7 Play a game in teams of four. Your teacher says an adjective. Which animals does it describe? Write a list. You have one minute. Which team has the longest list?
Teacher: *fast*
Group: *giraffe, elephant, …*

I can understand a text about animals.

7.6 Listening and Writing
Looking after a pet

1 In pairs, make a list of animals that you can have as pets. Then say which animals are easy to look after in your opinion.
Cats – easy. You don't take cats for a walk!

2 🔊 7.17 Listen to a radio interview with Jo, a pet expert. Tick (✓) the names of the animals on your list that you hear.

3 🔊 7.17 Listen again. Look and tick (✓) a, b or c.
1 Which animal is dangerous?
a ☐   b ☐   c ☐

2 What do dogs like?
a ☐   b ☐   c ☐

3 Which pet sleeps a lot?
a ☐   b ☐   c ☐

4 🔊 7.18 Listen to George talking about his new pet. Choose the correct option.
1 George's rabbit is *clever* / *boring*.
2 His favourite place is *his rabbit house* / *the garden*.
3 He eats *green* / *red and green* vegetables.
4 He drinks *water* / *milk*.
5 George has got *one rabbit* / *two rabbits*.

5 In pairs, talk about your ideal pet. What is it? What do you know about it?

6 Read Martin's email to Jen. What is it about? Choose the correct answer.
a his weekend   b his puppy

✉
Hi Jen,

Can you look after my puppy for the weekend? His name's Rex.

He eats dog food and he drinks water. He likes milk too. I take him for a walk after his breakfast and dinner. He sleeps a lot. He's very friendly and very cute!

Is this OK? Let me know.

Thanks,
Martin

7 Study the Writing box. How does the email begin? How does it end?

WRITING ▸ Starting and ending an email
Begin with *Hi* / *Hello*.
Write a comma after the name, e.g. *Hi Jen,* …
Write your name at the end, e.g. *Martin*

8 Order the sentences to make an email.
a ☐ She eats cat food and chicken. She drinks water.
b ☐ Helena
c ☐ Thanks,
d ☐ Is this OK? Let me know.
e ☐ 1 Hi Ben,
f ☐ Can you look after my cat for the weekend?

WRITING TIME
9 Write an email to a friend asking him/her to look after your pet.

1 Find ideas
Make notes about your pet.

2 Draft
Write *Hi* / *Hello* and your friend's name.
Explain why you are writing.
Can you look after my … for the weekend?
Give helpful information.
He/She eats/drinks/likes/sleeps …
End your email.
Is this OK? Let me know.
Thank your friend and write your name.

3 Check and write
Check the beginning and ending of your email.
Write the final version of your text.

7.7 CLIL: Science
The environment

1 🔊 **7.19** Listen and repeat. Match the phrases in the Vocabulary box with photos 1–6.

> **VOCABULARY** — **Where animals live**
>
> in the forest ☐   in a hole in the ground ☐
> on land ☐   in a pond ☐   in the sea ☐   in trees ☐

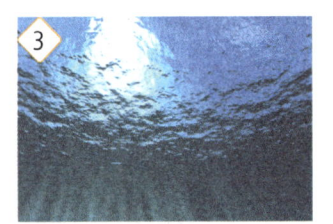

2 Read the texts. Match headings a–b with texts 1–2.

a Water animals   b Land animals

1 _____

A lot of animals, like tigers, elephants, giraffes and butterflies, live in forests. There are many different types of forests all over the world.

Some animals live in trees. They can do that because they can climb or fly. Some of these animals are monkeys, snakes, birds and spiders.

Rabbits make holes in the ground and they make a lot of them! They live there with their friends and families.

2 _____

There is a lot of life in ponds! Fish and frogs have their home there. Frogs are different from fish because they don't live only in the water. They can also live on land.

You can find a lot of different fish in the sea. They are big, small, cute, funny or ugly and they are many different colours. Whales live in the sea too.

3 Read the texts in Exercise 2 again. Mark the sentences T (true) or F (false).

1 All forests are the same.   T / F
2 Only birds live in trees.   T / F
3 Rabbits live together with other rabbits.   T / F
4 Fish don't live on land.   T / F
5 Fish can be many different colours.   T / F
6 Whales live in ponds.   T / F

4 What animals live in these places? Complete the table. Use information from the texts in Exercise 2.

1	In the forest	butterfly,
2	In trees	
3	In a hole in the ground	
4	In a pond	
5	In the sea	

5 Look at the animals in the photos. In pairs, guess where they live. Go to page 142 and check.

A: *Where do catfish live?*
B: *I think they live …*

catfish   fox   groundhog   octopus   koala

6 Add one more animal to the table in Exercise 4.

I can say and write where animals live.   **111**   Unit 7

Vocabulary Activator

WORDLIST 🔊 7.20

Wild animals
bird (n)
butterfly (n)
crocodile (n)
elephant (n)
fish (n)
fly (n)
frog (n)
giraffe (n)
kangaroo (n)
lion (n)
monkey (n)
snake (n)
spider (n)
tiger (n)
whale (n)

Pets
cat (n)
dog (n)
goldfish (n)

hamster (n)
iguana (n)
parrot (n)
rabbit (n)
tortoise (n)

Adjectives
cute (adj)
dangerous (adj)
fast (adj)
slow (adj)
strong (adj)
ugly (adj)

Where animals live
in a hole in the ground
in a pond
in the forest
in the sea
in trees
on land

Extra words
amazing (adj)
at 55 kilometres an hour
at the weekend
because (conjunction)
children (singular: child) (n)
dog food (n)
drink (v)
easy (adj)
every day
expert (n)
food (n)
foreign language
guide (n)
hard work
have fun
hour (n)
I could eat a horse!
I don't mind.
I'm allergic to

interview (n)
kilo (n)
leaves (singular: leaf) (n)
litre (n)
look after (v)
magazine (n)
night (n)
not … at all
Oh, all right.
pass (n)
Poor dog!
puppy (n)
relax (v)
reporter (n)
sleep (v)
take the dog for a walk
think (v)
together (adv)
water (n)
win (v)
work (v)

1 Look at pictures 1–8 and write the animals.

1 *elephant*
2 _____ 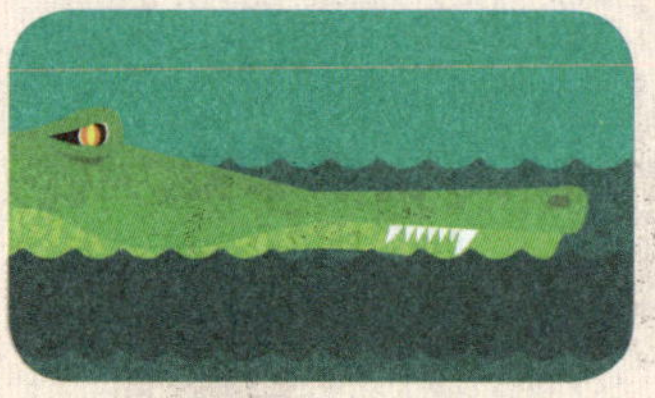
3 _____ 
4 _____ 
5 _____ 
6 _____ 
7 _____ 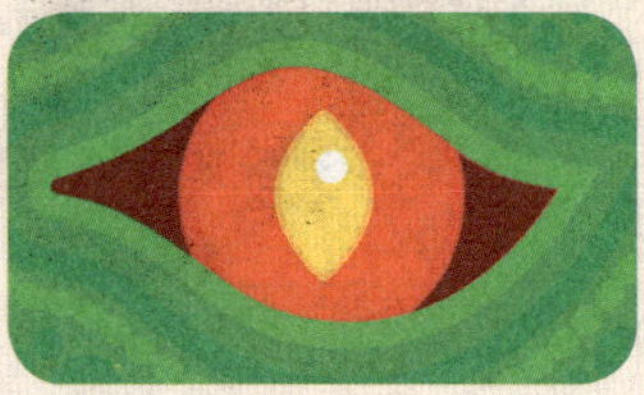
8 _____ 

2 Read the questions. Choose the correct answer.

1 Which animal is fast? *b*
   Which animal is slow? *a*
   a tortoise   b tiger
2 Which animal is strong? ___
   Which animal has got legs? ___
   a snake   b lion
3 Which animal is cute? ___
   Which animal is ugly? ___
   a cat   b fly
4 Which animal lives in a pond? ___
   Which animal lives in a tree? ___
   a bird   b frog
5 Which animal lives in people's houses? ___
   Which animal lives in a forest? ___
   a giraffe   b spider
6 Which animal lives in the sea? ___
   Which animal lives in a hole in the ground? ___
   a rabbit   b whale

3 🔊 7.21 **PRONUNCIATION** /s/
Listen and repeat.
Sue's **s**nake **S**imon ju**s**t eat**s**, eat**s** and eat**s**.
He **s**it**s** on the **s**ofa and **s**teals all the **s**weets!

Revision

Vocabulary

1 Choose the odd one out. Why is it different?
1. a bird   c butterfly
   b fly   (d) kangaroo
2. a crocodile   c snake
   b tiger   d elephant
3. a monkey   c fish
   b frog   d whale
4. a giraffe   c lion
   b spider   d tiger

2 How many pets can you see? Write the number.

1 cats *one*   5 tortoises _____
2 rabbits _____   6 iguanas _____
3 parrots _____   7 dogs _____
4 goldfish _____   8 hamsters _____

3 Complete the adjectives.
1 str o n g   4 sl __ __
2 danger __ __ __ 5 ug __ __
3 fa __ __   6 cu __ __

4 Complete the sentences with the words below.

| forest   ground   hole   land   pond   sea   trees |

1 Whales live in the *sea* and lions live on _____ .
2 Frogs live in a _____ .
3 Elephants and giraffes live in the _____ .
4 Monkeys and birds live in _____ .
5 Rabbits live in a _____ in the _____ .

Grammar

5 Read the text and write negative sentences in your notebook.

Jason and his family are very different!

Jason wants an iguana. His sister Jackie wants a rabbit, and their parents want a parrot.

They all watch TV. Jackie, Mum and Dad like films and Jason likes cartoons.

At the weekend, Jason goes to the park with his friends. Jackie hangs out with her best friend, and their parents visit the neighbours.

1 Jackie and Jason / want / a parrot
  Jackie and Jason don't want a parrot.
2 their parents / want / an iguana
3 Jackie / like / cartoons
4 Jason / go / to the park with his parents
5 his parents / go to the park

6 In your notebook, write questions and answers.
1 Jason / want / a rabbit?
  A: *Does Jason want a rabbit?*
  B: *No, he doesn't.*
2 his parents / want / an iguana?
3 they all / watch TV?
4 what / Jackie / do / at the weekend?
5 where / Jason / go / at the weekend?

Speaking

7 Choose the correct answer.
1 Can I help you?
  a Can I have a ticket, please?
  b Would you like a ticket?
2 That's ten pounds ninety.
  a The money's here.
  b Here you are.
3 Here are your tickets.
  a Thanks.
  b No, they aren't.

BBC CULTURE — Pets in the UK

1 Discuss these questions in class.
1 Which pets are popular in your country?
2 Do you know any unusual pets? What are they?
3 Would you like to have an exotic animal as a pet?

2 🔊 7.22 Listen and read. Match photos A–D with texts 1–3. There is one extra photo.

Pets in the UK
Some people in the UK want an unusual pet. This is why they choose exotic animals. Here are three unusual pets that you can have in the UK.

1 ☐ **Tarantulas**
Spiders are scary, but some people think tarantulas are pretty. They are quiet animals and they don't need a lot of space or food, so they aren't hard work.

2 ☐ **Pygmy hedgehogs**
People like pygmy hedgehogs because they are small and cute. They eat cat food and they eat a lot! They need a lot of space to run and play.

3 ☐ **Axolotls**
They've got an unusual name and they look funny. They live in the water. They can be brown, black, yellow, white or other colours. And here's an amazing fact: if they lose a part of their body, they can make a new one!

3 Read the texts in Exercise 2 again and answer the questions.
1 Which pet eats a lot?
The pygmy hedgehog.
2 Which pet can make new body parts?
3 Which pet needs a lot of space?
4 Which pet doesn't need a lot of food?
5 Which pet can be different colours?
6 Which pet can be scary?

4 🔊 7.23 Listen and choose the correct answer.
1 Which is the number one pet in the UK?
 a cat   b dog
2 Which animal is number three in the list?
 a rabbit   b fish
3 Which are two top names for pets in the UK?
 a Alfie and Bella   b Cookie and Dolly
4 What is their dog's name?
 a George   b Mrs C

5 Work in pairs. Imagine you can have one of the animals in photos A–D.
1 Which animal do you choose? Why?
2 Think of a name for your animal.

---

exotic (adj) interesting and unusual because it is from a foreign place
popular (adj) something is popular when a lot of people like or do it
unusual (adj) different from what we usually do or know

BBC ▶ London Zoo

6 ▶ 40 Watch the video and answer the presenter's questions. What do the animals do after breakfast?

7 ▶ 40 Watch the video again. Match the animals below with sentences 1–6. Use the information from the video, not what you know.

monkeys   penguins   stick insects   tigers (×2)   tortoises

1 They're fast. _tigers_
2 They're slow. _____
3 They're green. _____
4 They eat fish. _____
5 They eat meat. _____
6 They love toys. _____

8 Discuss in groups. Which animals in London Zoo would you like to see? Why?

PROJECT TIME

9 In groups of three, make a digital presentation with photos and information about your ideal pets.

1 In your group, think of six ideal pets, two pets for each person in your group. Find information about them. Use these questions to help you.
- What animals are your ideal pets?
- What do they look like?
- What do they eat?
- What can they do?
- What is a fun fact about them?

2 Individually, create your part of the presentation.
- Make digital posters of the pets.
- Find photos of each pet.
- Write a short text about each pet.
- Give each text a title.

3 In your group, create your presentation.
- Put the photos and texts together.
- Think of a title for the whole presentation.
- Check that the texts are correct.

4 Share your presentation with the class.
- Present your pets.
- Answer other students' questions.
- Ask questions and comment on the other presentations.

- This is my pet *rabbit*.
- His/Her name's …
- He/She's *cute/clever*.
- He/She eats …
- He/She can …
- Here's a fun fact about *rabbits*: …

VOCABULARY
Sports | Healthy lifestyle | Sports equipment

GRAMMAR
love / like / don't like / hate + -ing | Object pronouns | Question words

I like that!

8

8.1 Vocabulary

Sports

1 Read the words below. What do they mean?

basketball   football   skateboarding   swimming   tennis   volleyball

Unit 8   116

2 🔊 8.1 Listen and repeat. Match the words in the Vocabulary box with photos A–Q on page 116. Which sport is in two photos?

> **VOCABULARY** Sports
>
> badminton   basketball   canoeing   cycling   football
> hockey   ice-skating   roller skating   skateboarding
> snowboarding   swimming   table tennis   taekwondo
> tennis   volleyball   windsurfing

3 Unscramble the words. Use the Vocabulary box to help you.
1. tekaodnwo — t a e k w o n d o
2. anngcioe — c _ _ _ _ _ g
3. rloerl kasitng — r _ _ _ _ _ r s _ _ _ _ _ _ g
4. sktbraoadenig — s _ _ _ _ _ _ _ _ _ _ _ g
5. swobonrdiang — s _ _ _ _ _ _ _ _ _ _ g
6. hoecky — h _ _ _ _ y
7. bsktbaelal — b _ _ _ _ _ _ _ _ l
8. bdatinmon — b _ _ _ _ _ _ _ n

4 In pairs, put the sports in the Vocabulary box in groups. A sport can be in more than one group.

Indoor sports: *basketball,* _____
Outdoor sports: *football,* _____ 
Team sports: _____ 
Winter sports: _____ 
Ball sports: _____ 
Water sports: _____ 

> **WATCH OUT!**
> I **do** taekwondo.
> I **go** swimming.
> I **play** tennis.

5 🔊 8.2 Complete the phrases with *go* or *play*. In pairs, compare your answers. Then listen and check.
1. *go* cycling
2. ____ basketball
3. ____ hockey
4. ____ snowboarding
5. ____ skateboarding
6. ____ roller skating
7. ____ windsurfing
8. ____ badminton
9. ____ table tennis
10. ____ canoeing
11. ____ football
12. ____ ice-skating

6 These children do two sports. Look at the pictures and complete the sentences.

Mario    Alicia
Peter    Fran 

1. Mario *plays badminton* at school.
   He _____ at the weekend.
2. Alicia _____ at school. She also _____ with her dad.
3. Peter _____ in the school team.
   He _____ every week.
4. Fran _____ in winter. She always _____ in the morning.

YOUR WORLD

7 Complete the sentences with verbs and sports from Exercise 5.
I never _____ .
I watch _____ on TV.
I think _____ is boring.
I think _____ is great!
I _____ with friends.
I _____ every day.
I often _____ at school.

I can talk about sports.

8.2 Grammar

love / like / don't like / hate + -ing Object pronouns

VIDEO ▶ LET'S GO TO SUMMER CAMP!

Lian: Hey, guys, do you want to go to summer camp with me?
Alex: Maybe. What do you do there?
Lian: Horse-riding, rock climbing … I like rock climbing.
Jen: I don't like it!
Lian: How about water sports? There's sailing, windsurfing …
Alex: No, thanks. I don't like getting wet.
Jen: That's true. Lian, you like sports. We like them, but we want to do other things too. Cooking, for example.
Lian: There's a cooking camp in …
Alex: No, thanks. I love eating, but I hate cooking!
Lian: Let's find a camp we all like.

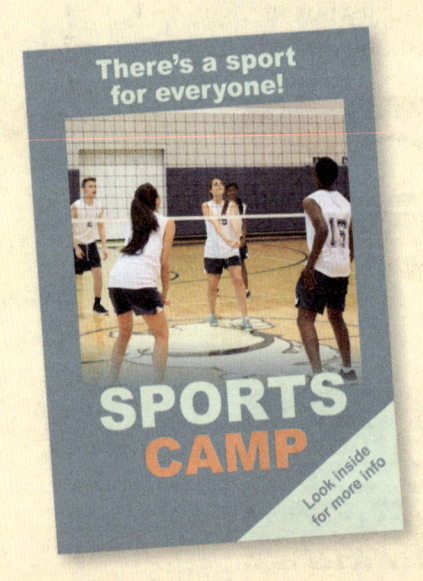

1 ▶ 41 🔊 8.3 Watch the video. Then listen and read. Find two sports in the story that are not in the Vocabulary box on page 117.

2 Read the story again. Complete the sentences with one word in each gap.
  1 Lian wants to go to <u>summer</u> camp.
  2 _____ doesn't like rock climbing.
  3 Sailing and windsurfing are _____ sports.
  4 Windsurfing is not a good sport for _____.
  5 Jen wants to go to a _____ camp, but Alex doesn't.

SOUNDS GOOD! Maybe. • That's true.

3 🔊 8.4 Listen and repeat. Find these expressions in the story.

4 Look at the summer camp brochures. Which camp is good for Lian, Jen and Alex? Choose the correct answer.
  a tech camp   b fun camp   c sports camp

5 ▶ 42 🔊 8.5 Now watch or listen and check.

Unit 8 118

6 Study the Grammar box. Then watch.

> **GRAMMAR** love / like / don't like / hate + -ing
>
> I love eating.   I hate cooking.
> I don't like getting wet.
>
> Do you like cycling? Yes, I do. / No, I don't.
> What do you like doing? I like cooking.

VIDEO ▶ 43 GET GRAMMAR!

Hammy hates getting wet!

7 Read the story on page 118 again. Complete the sentences with *loves, likes, doesn't like* or *hates*.
1 Jen _doesn't like_ rock climbing.
2 Lian _____ rock climbing.
3 Alex _____ getting wet.
4 Alex _____ eating, but he _____ cooking.

8 Look at photos 1–6. Write true sentences in your notebook. Use *love, like, don't like* or *hate* + *-ing*.

| cook   do homework   draw   get up   play   swim |

1 *I like playing computer games.*

9 🔊 8.6 Listen and mark the sentences T (true) or F (false).
1 Sue doesn't like playing volleyball.   T / F
2 Brian likes swimming.   T / F
3 Kate hates getting up early.   T / F
4 They love skateboarding.   T / F
5 Jake doesn't like playing football.   T / F

> **GRAMMAR** Object pronouns
>
> I → me   he → him   we → us
> you → you   she → her   you → you
>   it → it   they → them
>
> She is a good friend. I like her.
> You don't like sports. We love them.

10 Read Lian's email and choose the correct option.

My friend Alex loves fixing computers. ¹(He) / Him knows a lot of things about ²they / them. I don't, so I usually ask ³he / him for help. ⁴We / Us often hang out with his sister, Jen. I like ⁵she / her a lot. Jen loves making cupcakes. ⁶They / Them are amazing! Alex and I love chocolate, so ⁷she / her often makes chocolate cupcakes for ⁸we / us.

YOUR WORLD

11 Write what your friends or family *love/like/don't like/hate* doing. Use Lian's email in Exercise 10 to help you.

My friend … likes … . He/She knows a lot of things about …

I can use the verbs *love / like / don't like / hate* + *-ing* and object pronouns.

8.3 Grammar
Question words

The Terrific Two – Dug's sports hero

1
Dug: Excuse me, are you Irina Peters, the tennis player?
Irina: Yes, I am.
Dug: Can I have your autograph, please? I'm a great fan!
Irina: Sure. Hold my phone, please. What is your name?
Dug: Dug, erm … no … Superdug.
Irina: Are you THE Superdug?

2
Superdug: Yes. Look! Selfie?
Irina: Wow, yes! I'm your fan too!

3
Superdug: Here's your phone.

4
Kit: What have you got there?
Dug: It's Irina Peters' autograph.
Kit: She's a tennis champion! Well done, Dug!

5
Dug: And here's a photo of us. Oh, no! This isn't my pho[ne]
Kit: Whose phone is it?
Dug: It's Irina Peters' phone. We've got the same phone
Kit: Where can you find her? Where does she live?
Dug: I don't know.
Kit: I'm sure you're not her favourite superhero right n[ow]

1 Look at the cartoon. How many mobile phones can you see? What do you notice about them?

2 🔊 8.7 Listen and read. Who is Irina Peters?

3 Read the sentences. Mark them T (true) or F (false).
1 Irina wants Dug's autograph. T / F
2 Irina is Superdug's fan. T / F
3 Kit doesn't know who Irina Peters is. T / F
4 Dug's got the wrong phone. T / F
5 Dug doesn't know where his phone is. T / F

Unit 8 120

4 Study the Grammar box. Then watch.

GRAMMAR — Question words

Who is Dug's sports hero?	It's Irina Peters.
What have you got there?	I've got Irina's autograph.
When is the game?	It's on Tuesday.
Where does she live?	She lives in London.
Whose phone is it?	It's Irina's phone.
How many photos have you got?	I've got 80 photos.

VIDEO ▶ 44 GET GRAMMAR!

Where does she live?
She lives in Hong Kong.

5 Match questions 1–6 with answers a–f.
1 ☐ Where do Superdug and Kit live?   a Two.
2 ☐ Who is a tennis champion?   b Fish and chips.
3 ☐ How many sisters has Kit got?   c Irina.
4 ☐ When is Superdug's birthday?   d In the UK.
5 ☐ What is Kit's favourite dinner?   e Superdug's.
6 ☐ Whose bike is red and white?   f On 5 July.

6 How well do you know the Terrific Two? Complete the questions with the question words below. Then answer the questions in pairs.

how many   what   when   where   ~~who~~   whose

1 A: _Who_ is Uncle Roberto? (Look at page 16.)
  B: _He's Superdug's uncle._
2 A: _____ is in the box? (Look at page 30.)
3 A: _____ is Granny's house? (Look at page 46.)
4 A: _____ eyes are green? (Look at page 60.)
5 A: _____ children are there in the boat? (Look at page 76.)
6 A: _____ does Superdug play football? (Look at page 90.)

7 🔊 8.8 Listen to Superdug's questions. Then choose Kit's answers.

1 (On Wednesdays) / At her house.
2 Two cars. / I've got them.
3 In Spain. / You are.
4 It's my sister's. / Two sisters.
5 They're Wonder Will's. / I think there are four.
6 It's in your room. / It's nice.

8 Write questions about the underlined words.
1 A: _What is your favourite sport?_
  B: My favourite sport is rock climbing.
2 A: _____?
  B: My favourite sportsperson is Rafael Nadal.
3 A: _____?
  B: I live at 6 Rose Street.
4 A: _____?
  B: My birthday is on 26 August.
5 A: _____?
  B: I've got one brother and one sister.

YOUR WORLD

9 In pairs, ask questions 1–5 from Exercise 8 and give true answers.
A: What is your favourite sport?
B: It's …

10 Play a game! Make questions with the words in the box. You have three minutes.

where	Jack	swim	is
does	can	when	what
whose	who	he	like

Where is Jack?
Where can Jack swim?

I can ask detailed questions.

8.4 Speaking
Talking about the weather

VIDEO ▶ WHAT'S THE WEATHER LIKE?

Lucas is on holiday in Spain, but it's rainy in London.

Jen: Hi, Lucas! Why aren't you at the beach? Isn't it hot and sunny?
Lucas: It's three o'clock. It's too hot and too sunny. What's the weather like in the UK?
Jen: It's cold and rainy. We can't go swimming.
Lucas: That's a pity.
Jen: Yes, but it's OK. It often rains in summer.
Lucas: Well, I hope it's sunny tomorrow.
Jen: Me too, but I still can't go swimming.
Lucas: Why?
Jen: I have a dentist's appointment!
Lucas: Eurgh! I hate dentists!
Jen: Me too!
Lucas: See you soon! Bye!

1 ▶ 45 ◀)) 8.9 Watch the video. Then listen and read. Complete the sentence.

Jen can't go swimming today because _____.

2 ◀)) 8.10 Listen and repeat.

> **SPEAKING** Talking about the weather
>
> A: What's the weather like?
> B: It's *cloudy/cold/hot/rainy/snowy/sunny/warm/windy*.
>   It's *cold/hot/rainy/sunny* in *winter/summer/autumn/spring*.

3 What is the weather like? Complete the sentences.

1 It's *rainy*.
2 It's _____. 
3 It's _____. 
4 It's _____.

4 Which months are in each season in your country?

January February March
April May June July
August September October
November December

1 Summer: _____
2 Spring: _____
3 Winter: _____
4 Autumn: _____

5 Choose the best answer.
1 A: What's the weather like in autumn in Spain?
   B: a It's warm and sunny.
      b I like sunny weather.
2 A: I want to go windsurfing tomorrow.
   B: a Yes, it's cold.
      b I hope it's warm and windy.

YOUR WORLD

6 Play a game! Student A, say what the weather is like. Student B, suggest a sport you can do. Then change roles.

A: *It's windy.*
B: *Let's go windsurfing!*

Unit 8 · 122 · I can talk about the weather.

8.5 Reading and Vocabulary
Healthy lifestyle

1 🔊 8.11 Listen and repeat. Then match the phrases in the Vocabulary box to photos a–f in the magazine article below.

> **VOCABULARY** ▸ **Healthy lifestyle**
>
> brush your teeth   do exercise
> drink a lot of water   eat fruit and vegetables
> go to bed early   have friends

1 Photo a: _____
2 Photo b: _____
3 Photo c: _____
4 Photo d: _____
5 Photo e: _____
6 Photo f: _____

2 🔊 8.12 Read and listen to the magazine article. Match headings A–F with tips 1–6.
  A Healthy teeth   D People you like
  B Be sporty   E Healthy food
  C Sleep well   F Water is great!

3 Read the article again. Complete the sentences with one word in each gap.
  1 It's good to *get* up at the same time every day.
  2 Healthy teens eat fruit and _____ every day.
  3 Healthy teenagers drink a lot of _____.
  4 It's good to brush your _____ after every meal.
  5 When you want to exercise, you can play a sport, ride your bike or _____.
  6 It's fun to _____ out with friends.

4 Read the sentences. Tick (✓) the things that are healthy and put a cross (✗) if they are unhealthy.
  1 I sleep five hours every night.   ✗
  2 I never eat vegetables.   ☐
  3 I often brush my teeth after dinner but never after breakfast.   ☐
  4 I go swimming at the weekend.   ☐
  5 I meet my friends three times every week.   ☐

TEEN HEALTH — READ OUR TOP TIPS!

1 ☐ A healthy teenager needs nine hours of sleep. Go to bed early and get up at the same time every day.

2 ☐ Don't say 'I hate vegetables!' Find the fruit and vegetables you like. Eat five servings every day.

3 ☐ Healthy teenagers drink a lot of water. Have water in your schoolbag, not cola!

4 ☐ How often do you brush your teeth? Only after breakfast? Brush them after every meal, every day!

5 ☐ Do you like football, swimming or volleyball? Great! You don't? No problem! You can ride your bike or walk. It's good exercise!

6 ☐ Do you play computer games or watch TV after school on your own? Hang out with your friends sometimes. Friends are fun and they help us with our problems.

YOUR WORLD

5 Work in pairs. Talk about two healthy things that you do.
  I brush my teeth after every meal.

I can understand short texts about healthy habits.

8.6 Listening and Writing

Your lifestyle

1 Complete the sentences about sports champions with *train*, *good* and *healthy*.
1 Champions are _____ at their sport.
2 They _____ a lot.
3 They have a _____ lifestyle.

2 🔊 8.13 Listen to the interviews with Denise and Gary. What are their sports?

3 🔊 8.13 Listen again. Read the questions and complete the interviewer's notes about Denise and Gary.

Denise
1 Where does she play volleyball?
   At *City* Club.
2 When does she train?
   At _____ o'clock in the morning.
3 How often does she eat fruit and vegetables?
   Every _____ .
4 Has she got time for homework?
   _____ , she _____ .

Gary
5 How many friends has he got in his club?
   He's got _____ friends.
6 When does he train?
   From five to _____ every day.
7 When are his competitions?
   Usually on _____ mornings.
8 What does he always eat on Saturdays? _____ .

4 Have Denise and Gary got a healthy lifestyle? In pairs, compare your ideas.

5 Has Lucas got a healthy lifestyle? Read his blog and find out.

MY LIFESTYLE!

1 I go to bed at half past nine on school days and I get up at eight o'clock. I love sleeping!
2 My favourite food is pizza. Mum and Dad don't like pizza. Yes, really! They like fruit and vegetables. I drink a lot of water.
3 I'm not very sporty, but I like watching football on TV. I love music and I play the guitar every day after school.

6 Study the Writing box.

> **WRITING — Checking grammar**
> Read the first draft of your text to check for grammar mistakes. Check your final draft too.
> I like ~~watch~~ watching football on TV.

7 Correct the underlined mistakes.
1 I like <u>eat</u> chocolate.   *eating*
2 I hate swimming, but my friends like <u>him</u>.   _____
3 He <u>eat</u> a healthy breakfast.   _____
4 We love <u>do</u> sports.   _____

WRITING TIME

8 Write about your lifestyle.

1 Find ideas
Make notes under these headings.
Sleep: *I go to bed at …*
       I get up at …
Food: *My favourite food is …*
Sports and friends: *I am/I'm not very sporty.*
       I love/like/don't like/hate …
       I often/sometimes hang out with …

2 Draft
Write about your lifestyle.

3 Check and write
Check for grammar mistakes and write the final version of your text.

I can understand and write short texts about healthy lifestyles.

8.7 CLIL: Sports
Sports equipment

1 🔊 **8.14** Listen and repeat. Match the words in the Vocabulary box with the sports equipment A–F in the photos in Exercise 2.

VOCABULARY | Sports equipment

bat ☐   goggles ☐   helmet ☐   net ☐   racket ☐
stick ☐

2 What sports do the teens in the photos like? Complete the texts with the words below. There are four extra words.

badminton   ~~cycling~~   canoeing   hockey   snowboarding
swimming   table tennis   tennis   volleyball

YOUR WORLD

3 Complete the sentences so they are true for you.
I like _____ . I play/go _____ with _____ .
I need _____ to do this sport.

4 Complete the table with equipment words from the texts in Exercise 2.

Tennis	racket, ball, net
Hockey	
Volleyball	
Football	
Swimming	
Table tennis	
Cycling	

1 I love *cycling* because I can hang out with my friends outdoors. We ride our bikes at the weekend. I always wear a helmet.

2 I play _____ with my brother on Saturdays. You need a small ball and a bat for this sport. You play on a table with a net. There are usually two or four players.

3 I like _____ . I'm in a club. I train every day and I think I'm good at it. I wear goggles because I hate getting water in my eyes. I wear a swimming cap too because I've got long hair.

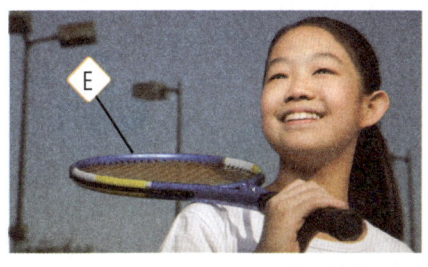

4 I love playing _____ . I often play with my sister. We play on Wednesdays and Fridays. I have a new racket. It's a birthday present.

5 I love playing ice _____ . You need a long stick to play, and it's also good to wear a helmet.

I can name sports equipment.   **125** Unit 8

Vocabulary Activator

WORDLIST 🔊 8.15

Sports
badminton (n)
basketball (n)
canoeing (n)
cycling (n)
football (n)
hockey (n)
ice-skating (n)
roller skating (n)
skateboarding (n)
snowboarding (n)
swimming (n)
table tennis (n)
taekwondo (n)
tennis (n)
volleyball (n)
windsurfing (n)

Healthy lifestyle
brush your teeth
do exercise
drink a lot of water
eat fruit and vegetables
go to bed early
have friends

Sports equipment
bat (n)
goggles (n)
helmet (n)
net (n)
racket (n)
stick (n)

Extra words
appointment (n)
at the beach
autograph (n)
champion (n)
chocolate (n)
cloudy (adj)
cold (adj)
competition (n)
fan (n)
find (v)
for example
from … to …
get wet
hate (v)
health (n)
healthy (adj)
horse-riding (n)
hot (adj)
I hope …
in the morning
Maybe.
meal (n)
pizza (n)
rainy (adj)
right now
rock climbing (n)
snowy (adj)
sporty (adj)
spring (n)
summer (n)
summer camp (n)
sunny (adj)
That's a pity.
That's true.
tip (n)
want (v)
warm (adj)
water sport (n)
Well done!
What's the weather like?
whose (pronoun)
windy (adj)
winter (n)

1 For which sport(s) do you need the equipment in pictures 1–8?

1 *cycling*
2 _____
3 _____
4 _____
5 _____
6 _____
7 _____
8 _____

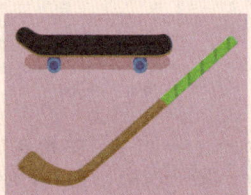

2 Find the words for sports equipment in the wordlist. Four of them are in the pictures in Exercise 1. Which two pieces of equipment are not in the pictures? Write them. Then draw them in the box.

_____ , _____

3 The underlined words are in the wrong phrase. Put them in the correct phrase.
For a healthy lifestyle:
1 brush your <u>water</u>   *teeth*
2 do <u>teeth</u>   _____
3 drink a lot of <u>early</u>   _____
4 eat fruit and <u>friends</u>   _____
5 go to bed <u>exercise</u>   _____
6 have <u>vegetables</u>   _____

4 🔊 8.16 **PRONUNCIATION** /r/
Listen and repeat.
Rosemary and Jane
Love running in the rain!

Unit 8 126

Revision

Vocabulary

1 Read sentences 1–5. Then complete the words for the sports.
  1 You play these sports with a ball.
    a b<u>asketball</u>
    b t_____ t_____
    c t_____
  2 These are not team sports.
    a r_____ s_____g
    b sk_____g
    c t_____
    d sn_____g
  3 You do these sports indoors and outdoors.
    a h_____
    b v_____
    c c_____
    d b_____
    e s_____
  4 You do these sports in winter.
    a sn_____g
    b i_____ - s_____
  5 You need windy weather for this sport.
    a w_____

2 Jamie's lifestyle isn't healthy. Give him some tips. Complete the sentences with the words below.

> bed   ~~exercise~~   friends   teeth   vegetables   water

  1 Do <u>exercise</u> every day.
  2 Eat fruit and _____ .
  3 Drink a lot of _____ .
  4 Brush your _____ after you eat.
  5 Hang out with your _____ .
  6 Go to _____ early.

3 Read the sentences. Mark them T (true) or F (false).
  1 You need a net to play volleyball.   T / F
  2 You don't need a bat to play table tennis. T / F
  3 You play badminton with a stick.   T / F
  4 You need a helmet to swim.   T / F
  5 It's good to wear goggles under water.   T / F
  6 You play tennis with a racket.   T / F

Grammar

4 Complete the text about Jamie with the correct form of the verbs in brackets.

Jamie isn't very sporty. He doesn't like ¹<u>doing</u> (do) sports at school and he doesn't like ²_____ (play) football with his friends. He ³_____ (hate) cycling too. He sometimes ⁴_____ (go) roller skating with his sister. They like ⁵_____ (go) to the park, but not when it's cold and rainy. Jamie loves ⁶_____ (watch) sports on TV at home!

5 Write questions. Then ask and answer in pairs.
  1 what / be / your favourite sport?
    What's your favourite sport?
  2 who / be / your sports hero?
  3 whose / autograph / you / have got?
  4 where / you / exercise? Indoors or outdoors?
  5 when / you / go to bed?
  6 how many friends / you / have got?

6 Read the sentences. Replace the underlined object pronouns with the words below.

> chocolate   Mr Smith   those roller skates
> you and me   ~~your mum~~

  1 I like <u>her</u>.   *your mum*
  2 I don't like <u>them</u>.   _____
  3 I love <u>it</u>!   _____
  4 They like <u>him</u>.   _____
  5 She can help <u>us</u>.   _____

Speaking

7 Match 1–4 with a–d.
  1 What's the weather   a in summer in the UK.
  2 It's sunny, but it's   b the UK in winter.
  3 It's often rainy   c windy.
  4 It's sometimes cold in   d like in the UK today?

SET FOR LIFE

I'm sorry, it's my fault!

A ☐

B ☐

C ☐

D ☐

1 Match 1–4 with photos A–D above.

1 Ron: Hang on! We're at 4, Rose Street. You say it's the address of the bookshop, but it isn't. This is an ice cream shop.
 Olga: Oh, no! I've got the wrong address!
2 Peter: Have you got our tickets?
 Haley: They aren't in my bag! They're at home!
3 Mr Reed: You're late! You play the drums in the school band and they can't start without you!
4 Nick: We're hungry, Sue! Is dinner ready?
 Sue: No, it isn't. It's on the floor!

2 Are you ever in situations like those in photos A–D? Read sentences a–e and tick (✓) the things you do.
 a ☐ I make mistakes.
 b ☐ I break things.
 c ☐ I forget things or I lose them.
 d ☐ I'm late.
 e ☐ I don't do the things people ask me to do.

3 Answer the questionnaire. Then compare your answers in pairs. Check your score on page 142.

How do you deal with mistakes?

1 You borrow your friend's laptop computer. It stops working.
 a You give it back and you say: 'There's something wrong with it. How can I fix it?'
 b You don't tell him. When he finds out, you say: 'I don't know anything about it.'
 c You don't tell him. When he finds out, you say: 'I'm sorry.'

2 You are working on a school project in a group. You don't do your part of the project well. The project gets a bad mark.
 a You tell the group: 'It's your fault.'
 b You tell the teacher: 'It's my fault.'
 c You tell the group: 'I'm sorry.'

3 You buy cinema tickets online for you and your friends. You make a mistake and buy tickets for the wrong time.
 a You say: 'I'm sorry.' Then you ask your friends to pay for the new tickets.
 b You say: 'There's a problem with the site.'
 c You say: 'I'm sorry.' Then you pay for new tickets for the right time.

4 Your mum texts you from work. She asks you to tidy the living room. You forget. Your mum comes back home with a friend and the living room is a mess.
 a You say: 'I'm sorry.' Then you tidy the living room quickly.
 b You say: 'I haven't got my phone with me.'
 c You promise to tidy the living room next time.

Reacting to mistakes

4 Look at the people A–D again. Then read 1–4 below and choose the best option.

1. Sue: I'm so sorry! It's my fault!
   Nick: *Why can't you be careful? / Don't worry, Sue. Accidents happen!*
   Sue: Let's order some pizza. My treat!
2. John: I'm really sorry, Mr Reed. How can I make up for it?
   Mr Reed: *Well, you can't! / Just don't be late next time.*
   John: I promise, Mr Reed.
3. Haley: I feel so bad about this!
   Peter: *It's your fault! We can't go to the zoo now! / Don't feel bad, Haley! I forget things too. Let's ask the people at the zoo. Maybe they can do something.*
4. Olga: *It's my mistake! / It isn't my fault!*
   Ron: That's OK. These things happen.
   Olga: *Can I buy you / Can you buy me* some ice cream to make up for it?
   Ron: That's a great idea!

5 🔊 8.17 In pairs, compare your answers to Exercise 4. Did you choose different answers? Why? Then listen and check.

6 In pairs, act out a complete dialogue from Exercise 1 or Exercise 4.

SET FOR LIFE

7 In pairs, write, act out and film a video clip about how to deal with situations like the ones in Exercise 2. Follow these steps.

1. Choose a situation from Exercise 2. Think of the details, e.g. who the people are, what happens.
2. Write your dialogue. Read the Useful Tips and use expressions from the Useful Phrases box.
3. Act out and film the dialogue.
4. Play the video clip to the class.

USEFUL TIPS

It's important to apologise for your mistakes. It's also important to be kind to people who make mistakes.

- Say sorry when you make a mistake.
- Do something nice to make up for your mistake.
- Don't let people feel bad about their mistakes.
- Help them to make things right again.

USEFUL PHRASES

What to say when you make a mistake.
- I'm so/very sorry.
- It's my fault.
- I feel so bad about this!
- How can I make up for it?

What to say to someone who makes a mistake.
- That's OK.
- Don't worry!
- Don't feel bad about it.
- These things happen.

I can react to mistakes.

Progress Check Units 1-8

Vocabulary and Grammar

1 Match categories A–F with words and phrases 1–6. Then add one more word or phrase to each category.

A Household objects
B Musical instruments
C Parts of the body
D Sports equipment
E Things we do to relax
F Women in the family

1 ☐ cushion, fridge, sofa, _____
2 ☐ mother, sister, aunt, _____
3 ☐ arm, nose, hair, _____
4 ☐ piano, drums, guitar, _____
5 ☐ listen to music, watch TV, play a game, _____
6 ☐ goggles, helmet, bat, _____

2 Find the words.

1 A sport like tennis, but with a different type of ball. (noun) *table tennis*
2 This very big animal lives in the sea, but it isn't a fish. (noun) _____
3 Not fast. (adjective) _____
4 You do this to make your bedroom look nice. (verb) _____
5 We cook our meals in this room. (noun) _____
6 You wear these on your feet when you do sports. (noun) _____
7 The day after the weekend. (noun) _____
8 It's good to do this in the morning and after meals. (three words) _____
9 A room usually has four of them. (noun) _____

3 Complete the dialogue with one word in each gap.
Kai is a new student at Alice's school.

Kai: ¹ *Have* you got a favourite cousin, Alice?
Alice: Yes, I have. ² _____ name's Emily.
Kai: ³ _____ does she live?
Alice: She ⁴ _____ in Southend. Her house is next ⁵ _____ the beach.
Kai: ⁶ _____ she go swimming?
Alice: No, she ⁷ _____ . She ⁸ _____ swim.
Kai: That's a pity! Swimming is a nice sport.
Alice: Emily does a lot of other sports. She ⁹ _____ hockey, tennis and football. She also loves singing. She ¹⁰ _____ music lessons after school.
Kai: I love music too! Is ¹¹ _____ a music club in our school?
Alice: Yes, there is. We ¹² _____ music lessons every Tuesday and Thursday.
Kai: That's fantastic!

Listening

4 🔊 8.18 Listen and match names 1-4 with pictures A-F. There are two extra pictures.
1 ☐ Beatrice   3 ☐ Mel
2 ☐ Charlie   4 ☐ Jeff

A B C D E F

Speaking

5 Read the answers and complete the questions.
1 A: Have *you got any tickets for the concert?*
   B: Yes, we have. There are a lot of tickets.
2 A: Can _____?
   B: Yes, sure. Three tickets are £27, please.
3 A: Where _____?
   B: It's June, so the concert is in the park.
4 A: Can _____?
   B: Yes, you can buy CDs at the concert.
5 A: What time _____?
   B: At eight o'clock.

6 In pairs, make mini dialogues. Then act them out.
1 What do you do to relax?
2 What do you say when someone apologises to you?
3 What's the weather like in winter in your country?
4 You and your friends want to hang out this afternoon. Make a suggestion.

Reading and Writing

7 In pairs, look at photos A–C. What sports do you use the equipment in?

SPORTS WEEK

What sports do you like?
What's your favourite sport? Write and tell us!

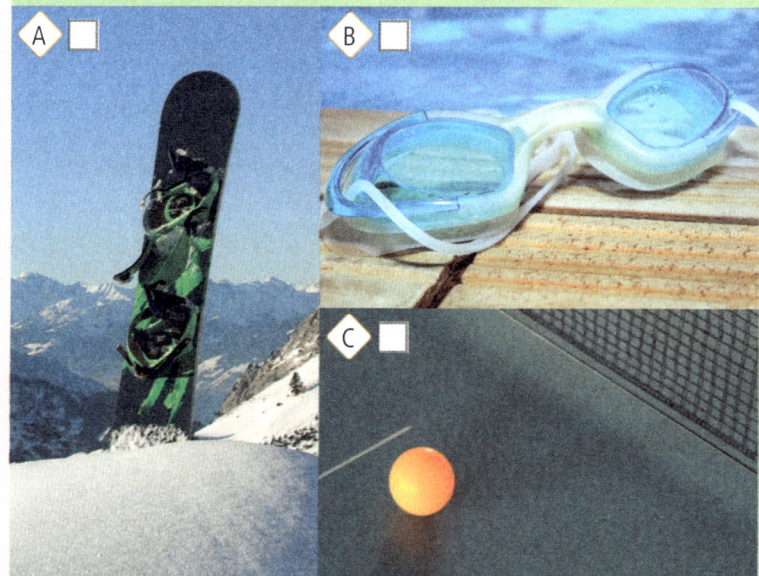

A ☐   B ☐   C ☐

1 I'm not usually very sporty. I hate team sports and I don't like water sports. But there's one sport I love: table tennis! I think I'm really good at it.

I play every day at school with my school friends in summer and in winter. I play in school competitions too. I usually win! *Jill, 12*

2 I'm in a football club and I play hockey, but my favourite sport isn't a ball sport. It's snowboarding.

There are some great places to snowboard in my country, Argentina. I always go snowboarding in August with my family. Yes, August! It's winter here in August. *Rod, 13*

3 My best friend and I go canoeing in summer. It's fun, but my number one sport is swimming.

I go to the swimming pool on Mondays and Fridays after school with my swimming club. I don't often swim in the sea. The water is very cold in Scotland! *Alistair, 14*

8 Read texts 1–3 and match them with photos A–C.

9 Read the texts again and complete the table.

	Jill	Rod	Alistair
What's his/her favourite sport?	table tennis		
Where does he/she do it?			
Who does he/she do it with?			

10 Read this. Choose a word from below. Write the correct word next to numbers 1–5. There are two extra words.

My ⁰*body* and head are orange and black. I see with my two yellow ¹_____. My four ²_____ are very strong. I've got big teeth and I am dangerous. I can run very fast! I don't eat fruit and ³_____. I eat meat. I like the ⁴_____, but I don't like very hot weather. Do I like ⁵_____? Yes, I like water! What am I? I am a tiger.

body   sun

man    swimming

eyes    vegetables

teeth    legs

11 Write a short description of an animal. Don't write its name. Can your teacher guess the animal?

12 Write 40–50 words about your favourite sport. Use these questions to help you.
1 What is your favourite sport?
2 Where and when do you do it?
3 Do you do it alone or with other people/in a team?
4 Are you good at it?
5 How often do you win?

Grammar Time

1.2
to be affirmative

Long form	Short form
I am happy.	I'm happy.
You are happy.	You're happy.
He/She/It is happy.	He/She/It's happy.
We are happy.	We're happy.
You are happy.	You're happy.
They are happy.	They're happy.

We often use the short form when we speak or write something informal.

1 Rewrite the sentences. Use the short form of the verb *to be*.
1. Melissa is thirteen years old.
   Melissa's thirteen years old.
2. They are cousins.
3. It is a birthday cake.
4. We are at my house now.
5. I am very happy!

2 Choose the correct option.
1. (She) / You is ready.
2. We / It are in Spain!
3. My name / I am Ben.
4. They / He are at Greg's house.
5. It / You is a present for you!
6. You / I are fourteen.

3 Write the dialogue in your notebook. Use the correct form of the verb *to be*.

Jackie: Hi! ¹my name / be / Jackie
My name's Jackie.
Liam: Oh, hi, Jackie. ²you / be / Nicki's friend, right?
Jackie: ³yes, I / be
Liam: ⁴I / be / Liam. ⁵Nicki and I / be / cousins
Jackie: Great! Here's some cake. ⁶today / be / my birthday
Liam: Happy birthday, Jackie!

4 Complete the text about yourself. Use the correct form of the verb *to be*.

Hi, my name's ¹_____ . Today I ²_____ years old. My friends and I ³_____ ready for my birthday cake. It ⁴_____ a lovely cake! Look at all the presents! They ⁵_____ for me!

1.3
to be negative

Long form	Short form
I am not fourteen.	I'm not fourteen.
You are not fourteen.	You aren't fourteen.
He/She/It is not fourteen.	He/She/It isn't fourteen.
We are not fourteen.	We aren't fourteen.
You are not fourteen.	You aren't fourteen.
They are not fourteen.	They aren't fourteen.

We add *not* after the verb *to be* to make it negative.
For the short form, join *are/is* and *not*: *aren't, isn't*.
For the first person, join *I* and *am*: *I'm not*.

1 Write *not* in the correct place to make the verb *to be* negative.
1. John _____ is *not* Tom's _____ uncle.
2. I _____ am _____ British.
3. They _____ are _____ from _____ France.
4. It _____ is _____ my _____ dog.
5. You _____ are _____ at _____ home.

2 Write negative sentences. Use the short form of the verb *to be*.
1. we / hungry — *We aren't hungry.*
2. she / happy _____
3. I / a superhero _____
4. he / here _____
5. you / in the photo _____
6. it / my name _____

3 Look at the table. Write true sentences. Use the affirmative or negative form of the verb *to be*.

	Jeanette	Ollie	Marcos	Mei Lin	Mel
Spanish	✗	✗	✓	✗	✓
Chinese	✗	✗	✗	✓	✗
French	✓	✗	✗	✗	✗
American	✗	✓	✗	✗	✗

1. Jeanette / Spanish
   Jeanette isn't Spanish.
2. Ollie / American
3. Marcos and Mei Lin / American
4. Mei Lin / French
5. Marcos and Mel / Spanish
6. Jeanette / Chinese

2.2

this, that, these, those

This is a blue T-shirt.	That is my dad's coat.
This T-shirt is blue.	That coat is my dad's.
These are Jenny's jeans.	Those are new shoes.
These jeans are Jenny's.	Those shoes are new.

We use *this/these* to talk about someone or something that is near.

We use *that/those* to talk about someone or something that is further away.

This/That = singular. *These/Those* = plural.

When we say that something is *here*, it is near us.

When we say that something is *there* or *over there*, it is away from us.

1 Rewrite the sentences.

1. These are Mum's trainers.
   These <u>trainers are Mum's</u>.
2. That is a lovely dress!
   That _____
3. This is a cool top.
   This _____
4. Those are Mark's trousers.
   Those _____
5. These are Sam's clothes.
   These _____
6. That is Carla's backpack.
   That _____

2 Write sentences. Use *this, that, these* or *those* and the words in the order they appear.

Here	There
long / skirt	short / skirt
jeans / blue	jeans / black
new / shoes	old / shoes
jacket / big	jacket / small
tracksuits / boring	tracksuits / cool
my favourite / trainers	trainers / my sister's

1. <u>This is a long skirt. That is a short shirt.</u>
2. _____
3. _____
4. _____
5. _____
6. _____

2.3

to be questions and short answers

?	Short answers
Am I a superhero?	Yes, I am. / No, I'm not.
Are you a superhero?	Yes, you are. / No, you aren't.
Is he/she/it a superhero?	Yes, he/she/it is. / No, he/she/it isn't.
Are we superheroes?	Yes, we are. / No, we aren't.
Are you superheroes?	Yes, you are. / No, you aren't.
Are they superheroes?	Yes, they are. / No, they aren't.
Wh- questions	**Full answers**
What is it?	It's a superhero suit.
Who are they?	They're my friends.

To ask a question with the verb *to be*, we change the position of *I/you/he/she/it/we/they* and *am/are/is*.
He is thirteen. – Is he thirteen?

We give a short answer to *yes/no* questions **only**.
A: Are you OK? B: Yes, I am.

We give a full answer to questions with *what, who*, etc.
A: Who is Harry? B: He's my best friend.

1 Write questions with the correct form of the verb *to be*.

1. you / at home?   <u>Are you at home?</u>
2. we / OK now?   _____
3. he / sorry?   _____
4. it / a new T-shirt?   _____
5. the cupcakes / for me? _____

2 Answer the questions in Exercise 1. Use short answers.

1. ✗ <u>No, I'm not.</u>
2. ✓ _____
3. ✓ _____
4. ✗ _____
5. ✓ _____

3 Complete the questions. Use *who* or *what* and the correct form of the verb *to be*.

1. <u>Who is</u> Peter? Peter is Mary's friend.
2. _____ it? It's my new jacket.
3. _____ these clothes? They're tracksuits.
4. _____ these boys? They're my classmates.

Grammar Time 133

Grammar Time

3.2

there is/there are affirmative

+	There is (There's) a book on the desk. There are two phones on the table. There are some books next to the TV.

We use *there is/there are* to say that someone or something exists or is present.

We use *there is* with singular nouns. We use *there are* with plural nouns.

The short form of *there is* is *there's*. There is no short form for *there are*.

With *there is/there are*, before plural nouns and uncountable nouns, we use *some* in affirmative sentences.

1 Choose the correct option.
1. There is *some books* / *a book* on my desk.
2. There's *a dog* / *two dogs* on a bike in the video!
3. There are some *orange juice* / *oranges* in the fridge.
4. There is *a poster* / *posters* on the wall.
5. There are *a window* / *two windows* in the kitchen.

2 Make the sentences singular or plural.
1. There's a bike in the garage.
   There are some bikes in the garage.
2. There are four chairs in the kitchen.
   _____
3. There's a window in the living room.
   _____
4. There are some sweets in my bag.
   _____

3 Match 1–6 with a–f and say where the things are. Then write sentences with *there's* or *there are*.

1	a bath	☐	a	in the house
2	four bedrooms	☐	b	in the fridge
3	some trees	☐	c	in the garage
4	a car	☐	d	in the wall
5	some milk	☐	e	in the bathroom
6	a window	☐	f	in the garden

1. *There's a bath in the bathroom.*
2. _____
3. _____
4. _____
5. _____
6. _____

3.3

there is/there are negative and questions

–	There isn't a tree in the garden.	There aren't any cars in the street.
?	Is there a tree in the garden? Yes, there is. / No, there isn't.	Are there any cars in the street? Yes, there are. / No, there aren't.

To ask a question, we change the position of *there* and *is/are*.
There is a cat on the bed. – *Is there* a cat on the bed?

We use *any* with plural nouns in questions and negative sentences.
Are there *any* cars in the street?
There aren't *any* cars in the street.

1 Write negative sentences.
1. white house in this street
   There isn't a white house in this street.
2. books on the desk
3. TV in my bedroom
4. chair in the garden
5. people in the house

2 Complete the sentences with *a* or *any*.
1. Are there *any* pictures in the living room?
2. There isn't _____ bath in this bathroom.
3. Is there _____ garage next to the house?
4. There aren't _____ bags on the floor.
5. Are there _____ oranges in the kitchen?

3 Write questions about an unusual house in your notebook. Then look at the table and answer the questions.

	bedroom	kitchen	bathroom	garage
bath	1	✗	✗	✗
sofas	✗	2	✗	✗
posters	✗	✗	10	✗
fridge	✗	✗	✗	1

1. bath / in the bathroom?
   A: Is there a bath in the bathroom?
   B: No, there isn't.
2. sofas / in the kitchen?
3. posters / in the bedroom?
4. fridge / in the garage?
5. bath / in the bedroom?
6. posters / in the bathroom?

4.2

have got affirmative and negative

+ Short and long form	− Short and long form
I've (have) got brown eyes.	I haven't (have not) got brown eyes.
You've (have) got brown eyes.	You haven't (have not) got brown eyes.
He/She/It's (has) got brown eyes.	He/She/It hasn't (has not) got brown eyes.
We've (have) got brown eyes.	We haven't (have not) got brown eyes.
You've (have) got brown eyes.	You haven't (have not) got brown eyes.
They've (have) got brown eyes.	They haven't (have not) got brown eyes.

We use *have got* with *I/you/we/they*. We use *has got* with *he/she/it*. We add *not* between *have* and *got* to make the negative form.

1 Choose the correct option.
 1 (Those cats) / That cat have got blue eyes.
 2 Mr Lewis / My grandparents has got white hair.
 3 Ian / The boys have got curly hair.
 4 Chris and Eve / Sandra has got small feet.
 5 Those dogs / My dog has got long ears.

2 Write negative sentences about the wrong options in Exercise 1.
 1 *That cat hasn't got* blue eyes.
 2 _____ white hair.
 3 _____ curly hair.
 4 _____ small feet.
 5 _____ long ears.

3 Write affirmative or negative sentences.
 Look at photo 1 on page 58.
 1 Mrs Newman / brown hair
  Mrs Newman has got brown hair.
 2 Jen / a big bag
 3 Jen and Alex / sandwiches in their hands
 4 Jen and Alex / trainers

 Look at photo 4 on page 58.
 5 Jen / long hair
 6 Alex / long hair

4.3

have got questions and short answers

?	Short answers
Have I got a pet?	Yes, I have. No, I haven't.
Have you got a pet?	Yes, you have. No, you haven't.
Has he/she/it got a pet?	Yes, he/she/it has. No, he/she/it hasn't.
Have we got a pet?	Yes, we have. No, we haven't.
Have you got a pet?	Yes, you have. No, you haven't.
Have they got a pet?	Yes, they have. No, they haven't.

What have you got? I've got a pet hamster!
To ask a question, we change the position of *I/you/we/they/he/she/it* and *have/has*.
They have got super powers. –
Have they got super powers?
We don't use *got* in short answers.
A: *Have you got a pencil?* B: *Yes, I have.*

1 Complete the questions.
 1 A: He's got a red superhero suit.
  B: *Has he got* a blue superhero suit too?
 2 A: She's got a cat.
  B: _____ a dog too?
 3 A: They've got long legs.
  B: _____ long arms too?
 4 A: It's a funny robot! It's got big ears.
  B: _____ a big nose too?
 5 A: I've got a brother.
  B: _____ a sister too?

2 Answer the questions in Exercise 1.
 1 ✓ *Yes, he has.* 2 ✗ 3 ✓ 4 ✗ 5 ✓

3 Complete the questions. In pairs, swap notebooks and write true answers.
 1 A: _____ you got _____?
  B: _____
 2 A: _____ your best friend got _____?
  B: _____

Grammar Time 135

Grammar Time

5.2

can affirmative and negative

+	−
I can cook.	I can't cook.
You can cook.	You can't cook.
He/She/It can cook.	He/She/It can't cook.
We can cook.	We can't cook.
You can cook.	You can't cook.
They can cook.	They can't cook.

1 Unscramble the words and write what these people can do.
1. Carol *can sing.* — isgn
2. We _____ — mwis
3. Henry _____ — ecnad
4. The girls _____ — cta

2 Who or what can't do these things? Choose and write negative sentences.
1. elephants / people – jump
   Elephants can't jump.
2. parrots / I – fly
   _____
3. a dog / a pop star – sing
   _____
4. my cat / my teacher – read
   _____

3 Complete the sentences with the verb *can* or *can't* and the verbs in brackets.
1. I *can swim* (✓swim), but I *can't run* (✗ run) fast.
2. My mum _____ (✗ ride) a horse, but she _____ (✓ride) a bike.
3. You _____ (✗ sing), but you _____ (✓dance).
4. We _____ (✓play) computer games, but we _____ (✗ play) the guitar.
5. My uncle _____ (✓fix) things, but he _____ (✗ fix) computers.

4 What can you, your mum, your dad and your best friend do? What can't you, your mum, your dad and your best friend do? Write eight true sentences.
I can fix things. I can't sing. My mum can play football very well. She can't sing.

5.3

can questions and short answers

?	Short answers
Can I run fast?	Yes, I can. / No, I can't.
Can you run fast?	Yes, you can. / No, you can't.
Can he/she/it run fast?	Yes, he/she/it can. / No, he/she/it can't.
Can we run fast?	Yes, we can. / No, we can't.
Can you run fast?	Yes, you can. / No, you can't.
Can they run fast?	Yes, they can. / No, they can't.

What can you do? I can run fast.

To ask a question, we change the position of *can* and *I/you/he/she/it/we/they*.

They can play football. – *Can they play football?*

1 Match questions 1–6 with answers a–f.
1. Can Mike play the guitar? ☐
2. Can I dance well? ☐
3. Can a dog fly? ☐
4. Can you cook? ☐
5. Can Dan and Liz make posters? ☐
6. Can Sue run fast? ☐

a. No, I can't.
b. No, it can't.
c. No, she can't.
d. Yes, he can.
e. Yes, they can.
f. Yes, you can.

2 Write questions with the verb *can*. Then answer them.
1. you / read English books? (✓)
   A: Can you read English books?
   B: Yes, I can.
2. your granny / play computer games? (✓)
3. Samantha / ride a horse? (✗)
4. dogs / swim? (✓)
5. we / fly? (✗)

3 Answer the questions about you.
1. Can you cook?
2. Can your grandparents dance?
3. Can your mum and dad read Chinese?
4. Can your best friend run fast?

6.2
Present Simple affirmative

	+
I	get up at seven.
You	get up at seven.
He/She/It	gets up at seven.
We	get up at seven.
You	get up at seven.
They	get up at seven.

Most verbs add -s: (verb: play) He plays music.
(verb: hang out) She hangs out with her friends.
Verbs ending in -ch, -o, -ss, -sh and -x add -es:
(verb: watch) He watches TV.
(verb: go) She goes to school.
Verbs ending in consonant + -y cut the -y and add -ies:
(verb: fly) She flies to Rome.
(verb: tidy) He tidies his room.
The verb have becomes has.

We use the Present Simple to talk about a habit or something you do regularly.

1 Choose the correct option.
1. Adam go / **goes** to school.
2. We do / does our homework in the afternoon.
3. Lisa listen / listens to music in the evening.
4. My sister have / has lunch at school.
5. They tidy / tidies the house at the weekend.

2 Complete the text with the correct form of the verbs in brackets. Use the Present Simple.

Julia ¹*gets up* (get up) at seven in the morning. She ²_____ (have) breakfast and she ³_____ (go) to school. She ⁴_____ (have) lessons all morning. She ⁵_____ (do) her homework in the afternoon. In the evening, she ⁶_____ (play) computer games. On Saturday morning, she ⁷_____ (tidy) her room. On Saturday afternoon, she ⁸_____ (hang out) with her friends.

3 Write true sentences about you and your family. Use the words below.

I   my mum   my dad   my parents   my brother/sister
do   get up   go   hang out
have   play   tidy   watch

6.3
Adverbs of frequency

●●●●●	They always do their homework.
●●●●○	I am usually late.
●●●○○	She often plays the piano.
●●○○○	You sometimes get up late.
○○○○○	He never goes to the gym.

Adverbs of frequency (never, often, etc.) go between I/you/he/she/it/we/they and Present Simple verbs.
They usually have lunch at home.
Adverbs of frequency go after I/you/he/she/it/we/they and the verb to be.
She is never at home.
We use adverbs of frequency to say how often we do something.

1 Order the words to make sentences.
1. we / have / in the morning / lessons / always
   We always have lessons in the morning.
2. late for breakfast / she / often / is
   _____
3. sometimes / computer games / play / they
   _____
4. walk / usually / I / to school
   _____
5. are / never / you / at home on Sunday
   _____

2 Write sentences with the correct form of the Present Simple and the adverbs in bold.
1. I / listen to classical music **never**
   I never listen to classical music.
2. Timothy / have dinner at eight. **usually**
3. my friends and I / go to the park **often**
4. you / be late for school **never**
5. my cousin Dom / get up early **always**
6. Leslie and Nicola / play tennis **often**
7. we / hang out in the park **sometimes**

3 How often do you do these things? Write true sentences.
1. ride my bike to school
2. go to bed after twelve
3. watch TV in the morning
4. have orange juice with my breakfast

Grammar Time

Grammar Time

7.2
Present Simple negative

Long form	Short form
I do not like snakes.	I don't like snakes.
You do not like snakes.	You don't like snakes.
He/She/It does not like snakes.	He/She/It doesn't like snakes.
We do not like snakes.	We don't like snakes.
You do not like snakes.	You don't like snakes.
They do not like snakes.	They don't like snakes.

To make the negative form, we use *does not/doesn't* with *he/she/it*, but we don't add *-s* to the main verb.

1 Complete the sentences with *don't* or *doesn't*.
1. My sister *doesn't* like parrots.
2. We _____ go to bed early on Saturday.
3. You _____ like spiders.
4. My dog _____ eat a lot.
5. The boys _____ play football in the street.
6. I _____ visit my cousins every week.

2 Write negative sentences.
1. Granny plays computer games.
   Granny doesn't play computer games.
2. We have breakfast at six o'clock.
   _____
3. I hang out with my friend after school.
   _____
4. Rob goes to school at seven o'clock.
   _____
5. Mum and Dad watch TV in the morning.
   _____

3 Write affirmative (✓) or negative (✗) sentences.
1. my dad / like / rabbits ✓ but my mum / want / a pet in the house. ✗
   My dad likes rabbits, but my mum doesn't want a pet in the house.
2. small animals / eat / a lot ✗ but my hamster / eat / all the time! ✓
3. my sister / play / with our iguana ✓ but my brother / like / it ✗
4. tortoises / walk / fast ✗ and they / play / games ✗

7.3
Present Simple questions and short answers

?	Short answers
Do I play the guitar?	Yes, I do. / No, I don't.
Do you play the guitar?	Yes, you do. / No, you don't.
Does he/she/it play the guitar?	Yes, he/she/it does. / No, he/she/it doesn't.
Do we play the guitar?	Yes, we do. / No, we don't.
Do you play the guitar?	Yes, you do. / No, you don't.
Do they play the guitar?	Yes, they do. / No, they don't.

We form questions with *do* + *I/you/we/they* + main verb or *does* + *he/she/it* + main verb without *-s*.

1 Match questions 1–6 with answers a–f.
1. Do you want a pet? ☐
2. Does Fred play football? ☐
3. Does your cat like milk? ☐
4. Do parrots sing? ☐
5. Do I play the piano well? ☐
6. Does Katie speak Spanish? ☐

a. No, it doesn't. d. Yes, I do.
b. Yes, he does. e. No, you don't.
c. No, they don't. f. Yes, she does.

2 Write the questions.
1. A: you / speak / any foreign languages?
   Do you speak any foreign languages?
   B: I speak English and Spanish.
2. A: Clare / have / piano lessons?
   B: No, she has guitar lessons.
3. A: you and your brother / visit / your cousins?
   B: Yes, when we visit our grandparents.

3 Complete the short answers.
1. A: Do you ride your bike to school?
   B: No, *I don't*.
2. A: Does your brother eat a lot?
   B: Yes, _____.
3. A: Do your grandparents like pop music?
   B: No, _____.
4. A: Do you and your friends hang out on Saturday?
   B: Yes, _____.

8.2
love / like / don't like / hate + -ing

I love playing hockey. I hate getting up early.
Do you like swimming? Yes, I do. / No, I don't.
What does she like doing? She likes watching TV.
We use love (☺☺) or hate (☹☹) when we have strong feelings about something.

1 Write sentences in your notebook.
1 Elsie / ☺ / play / tennis
   Elsie likes playing tennis.
2 I / ☹ / do / homework
3 they / ☺☺ / fly
4 we / ☹☹ / study on Friday

8.2
Object pronouns

me	Your cat likes me.
you	I go to school with you.
him	We know him.
her	I can help her.
it	We love watching it.
us	Play with us.
you	These boxes are for you.
them	You love them.

We often use pronouns to avoid repeating the same words.
Who is this boy? Do you know him?

2 Complete the text with the words below.

him   her   it   me   them

I don't like skateboarding, but my friends love ¹*it*! I usually go with ² _____ to the skate park, but I just watch. My friend Alistair is really good. I love watching ³ _____ skateboard. His sister Lisa doesn't skate. So she hangs out with ⁴ _____ .
I like ⁵ _____ !

8.3
Question words

Who is Matt?	He's my cousin.
What do you eat for breakfast?	I usually eat pancakes.
When is the football game?	It's this Saturday.
Where are the girls?	They're at school.
Whose bag is this?	It's Mel's bag.
How many cats has she got?	She's got two cats.

1 Choose the correct question.
1 A: a Where do you play tennis?
      b When do you go to the gym?
   B: On Wednesday and Friday.
2 A: a How many oranges are there?
      b What have you got in this bag?
   B: Two, I think.
3 A: a Whose birthday is it?
      b Who is it?
   B: Mary's.
4 A: a Where does she go after school?
      b What does she do after school?
   B: She watches TV.

2 Complete the questions with question words.
1 A: *Where* does she live?
   B: In the UK.
2 A: _____ students are there in your class?
   B: Twenty-six.
3 A: _____ jacket is this?
   B: My dad's.
4 A: _____ do you usually go on holiday?
   B: In July.
5 A: _____ is that girl?
   B: She's George's sister.

3 Write the questions.
1 A: *How many pets have you got?*
   B: Three. I've got a dog, a cat and a hamster.
2 A: _____?
   B: They live in Newcastle.
3 A: _____?
   B: It's Nico's bike.
4 A: _____?
   B: Mrs Cole is our teacher.

Student Activities

Unit 0 **Lesson 0.3** Exercise 5

1
2
3
4
5
6

Unit 1 **Lesson 1.5** Exercise 6

Take turns. Describe the photos. Use the example to help you.

A: It's a mum, a dad and three sons. They're on holiday.
B: It's photo A.

A
B
C
D

Unit 2 **Lesson 2.3** Exercise 10

🔊 2.9 🔊 2.10 Kit's Rap

Is she clever?	Yes, she is.
Is she fun?	She's all that!
Is she the best?	Her name's Kit
Is she the one?	and she's a cool cat!

Now you rap. You can rap about a friend!

140 Student Activities

Unit 3 **Lesson 3.2** Exercise 12

Play a drawing dictation game. Describe one of the pictures A–D for your partner to draw.

A

B

C

D

Unit 3 **Lesson 3.3** Exercise 8

Play a memory game.
Student A, choose one of the pictures A–D above.
Close your book.
Student B, ask Student A questions.
Then change roles.

A: Picture A.
B: Chairs?
A: There are four chairs.

Unit 4 **Lesson 4.3** Exercise 10

🔊 4.8 🔊 4.9 Robots' Song

Have you got super ears?
Have you got super eyes?
  Yes, we've got superpowers,
  We are super guys!
Have you got super arms,
Or maybe a super nose?
  We have got super feet,
  And twenty super toes!
Have you got a super boat?
Have you got a bike?
  No, we've got a super car,
  And its name is Mike!

Unit 5 **Lesson 5.3** Exercise 10

🔊 5.9 🔊 5.10 Activities Rap

I can act, I can sing, I can draw a cat.
I can run, I can swim – can you do all that?

I can act, I can sing, I can draw a cat.
I can run, I can swim – I can do all that!

Now you rap. Use different activities you know.

Student Activities **141**

Student Activities

Unit 5 **Lesson 5.5** Exercise 5

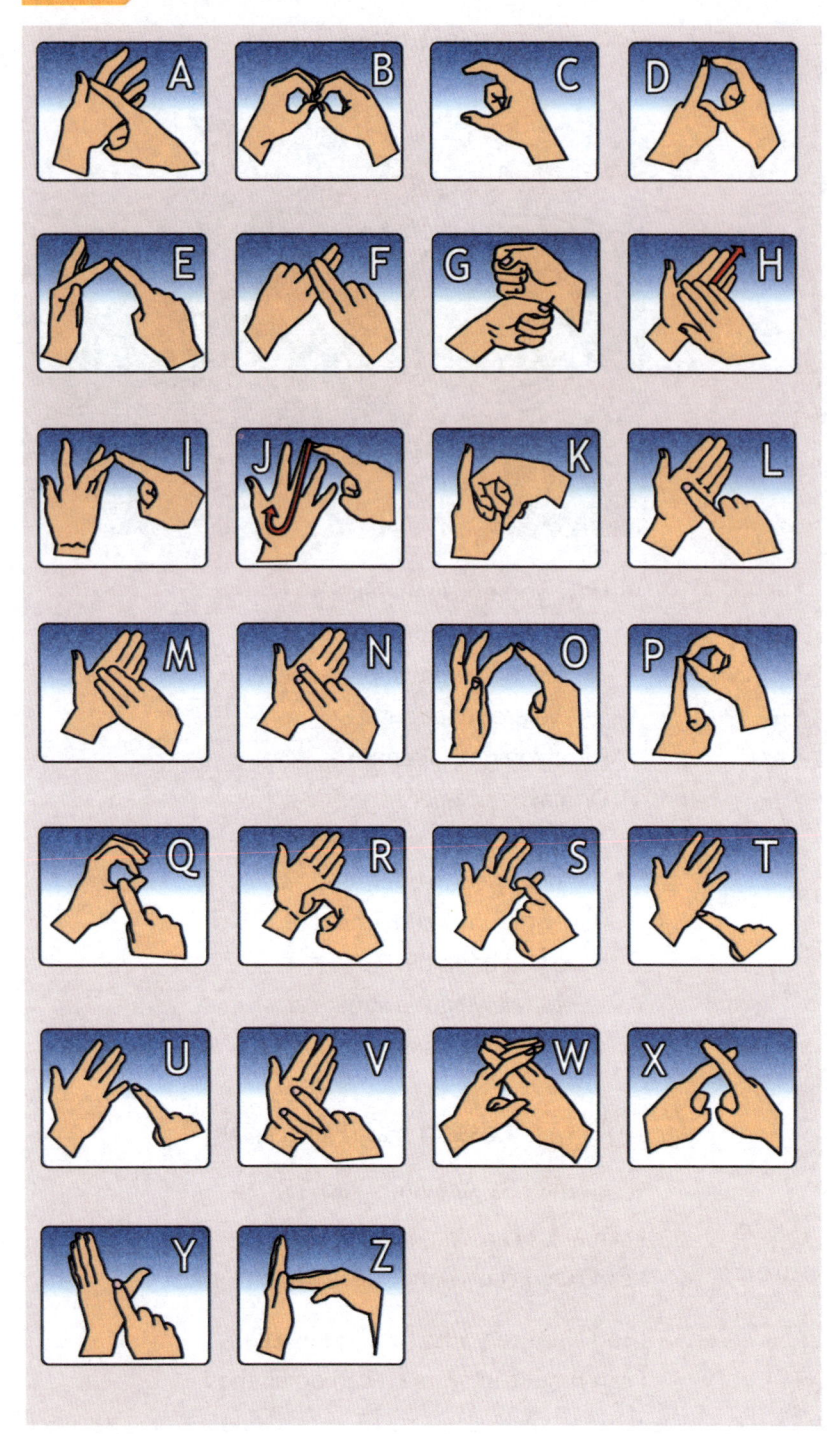

Unit 5 **Lesson 5.7** Exercise 2

1 F 2 T 3 F 4 F 5 F 6 F 7 T 8 T 9 T 10 F

Unit 7 **Lesson 7.2** Exercise 11

Student B
1 Alex wants to play with his pet.
2 Lucas doesn't like birds.
3 Lian's mum is allergic to cats and rabbits.

Student A
4 Granny wants to go for walks with her pet.
5 Aunt Megan loves birds.
6 Emma doesn't want a big pet.

Unit 7 **Lesson 7.3** Exercise 11

🔊 7.9 🔊 7.10 Questions Song

Do you play computer games?
Do you watch TV?
Do you hang out with your friends?
Then you're just like me!
Yes, you're just like me!

Does your mum say, 'Get up now!'?
Does she count to three?
Do you say, 'Oh, it's not fair!'?
Then you're just like me!
Yes, you're just like me!

Do you have your breakfast?
Do you go to school?
Do you like your English class?
Then you're really cool!
Yes, you're really cool!

Unit 7 **Lesson 7.7** Exercise 5

Catfish live in a pond. Foxes live in the forest. Groundhogs live in a hole in the ground. Octopuses live in the sea. Koalas live in trees.

Unit 8 **Set for life** Exercise 3

Score
1 a = 2 points; b = 0 points; 1 = 1 point
2 a = 0 points; b = 2 points; c = 1 point
3 a = 1 point; b = 0 points; c = 2 points
4 a = 2 points; b = 0 points; c = 1 points
0–3 points Not good at all! ☹
4–5 points You can do better. 😐
6–8 points You're good! 🙂